the definitive business pitch

the definitive business pitch

how to make the best pitches, proposals and presentations

ANGELA HATTON

An imprint of Pearson Education
Harlow, England • London • New York • Boston • San Francisco • Toronto • Sydney • Singapore • Hong Kong
Tokyo • Seoul • Taipei • New Delhi • Cape Town • Madrid • Mexico City • Amsterdam • Munich • Paris • Milan

PEARSON EDUCATION LIMITED

Edinburgh Gate
Harlow CM20 2JE
Tel: +44(0)1279 623623
Fax: +44(0)1279 431059
Website: www.pearsoned.co.uk

First published in Great Britain 2007

ISBN-13: 978-0-273-70826-1
ISBN-10: 0-273-70826-0

British Library Cataloguing-in-Publication Data
A catalogue record for this book is available from the British Library

Library of Congress Cataloging-in-Publication Data
Hatton, Angela.
The definitive business pitch : how to make the best pitches, proposals and presentations / Angela Hatton.
p. cm.
Includes index.
ISBN-13: 978-0-273-70826-1 (alk. paper)
ISBN-10: 0-273-70826-0 (alk. paper)
1. Business presentations–Handbooks, manuals, etc. 2. Proposal writing in business–Handbooks, manuals, etc. I. Title.

HF5718.22.H38 2006
658.4'5–dc22

2006051707

10 9 8 7 6 5 4 3 2 1
10 09 08 07 06

Microsoft product screen shots reprinted with permission from Microsoft Corporation.

Typeset in 9.5pt Stone Serif by 3
Printed and bound in Great Britain by Bell & Bain Ltd, Glasgow

The publishers' policy is to use paper manufactured from sustainable forests.

This book is dedicated to my sister, Rosalind, whose:

- love and support I appreciate more every year;
- personal courage and bravery leaves me speechless;
- commitment to starting a new career as an entrepreneur I admire.

I hope these ideas help make her new business, Footfocus Reflexology, a real success but I know her own dedication and caring skills will be the real keys to achieving her ambitions.

about the author

ANGELA HATTON

Angela Hatton is a specialist in writing, consulting and training on marketing strategy. She has more than 16 years' experience of pitching for training and consultancy for her own marketing and management business 'Tactics'. Over the years, her core clients have included Lloyds TSB, Norwich Union, IBM and City & Guilds. She has facilitated workshops on successful pitching and presentations for clients such as the BBC and IPC Media. Her previous publications include *The Definitive Guide to Marketing Planning.*

contents

preface

I know from personal experience – not always pleasant! – that pitches can be crucial in determining whether or not you win business. A while ago, I experienced a two-week period which, for one reason or another, was peppered with pitches, presentations and proposals. I endured some truly awful pitches from marketing teams who should have known better and some appallingly badly constructed ones from IT companies who didn't know how to present themselves and their work effectively. Needless to say, none of these teams or companies won the business. At the same time, I was working with a training-provider client to help improve its proposals while developing the usual clutch of presentations, pitches and proposals to feed my own business.

It was this intense exposure that made me think about how just a few simple tips and techniques can make so much difference to winning business – tips that I have used again and again with clients, who have gone on to improve their hit rates dramatically in winning business. This is why I decided to put this guide together, in order to share the tried and tested techniques I know can help you to do business more effectively.

I hope it helps you to review your own front-end client presentations and implement a few changes that will make a real difference to *your* business success.

Happy pitching!

Symbols used

 Tips – your shortcuts to success

 Activities – to get you thinking and doing

 In practice boxes – showing you real-world examples

acknowledgements

I must thank Dave who, for almost 30 years, has put up with me trying to juggle too many projects but who continues to do so with smiling support and love.

Thanks also to good friends Sylvia, who had the unenviable task of turning scribbles into a sensible script, and Fiona, who added the punctuation and spelling that helped make sense of my ramblings.

introduction

What's in it for you?

Like strangers in a lift, we don't know each other but I must try to convince you that I understand your needs. So can I persuade you? Let me start with what I know:

- Both at home and at work you find yourself having to present your ideas and plans.
- Increasingly you need to persuade others (internally and externally) to trust that you will deliver them benefits that outweigh the cost of your proposals.
- You do not necessarily consider yourself to be a sales or marketing professional. You may be an HR director making a business case internally for a new reward strategy, or part of a team who must pitch its consultancy or creative ideas to clients, or an author trying to sell a book idea to a publisher.
- The sales aspect of your work role is not your favourite part of the job.
- The process of selling your ideas and plans to others often makes you feel uncomfortable – you feel pushy or arrogant.
- You would prefer to let the quality of your ideas speak for themselves.
- The fact you have picked this book up shows you are aware that, in today's environment of choice, good ideas don't sell themselves.
- You are not successful as often as you should or could be.
- You sense that a few basic techniques and practical tips could help make a real difference to your success in pitching and winning proposals.

On the last point you are right – this book will take you through the process of structuring and presenting a pitch or proposal in a way which will help build your confidence in the process, and ensure that you will have more occasions to celebrate successes. You can expect to hear others saying 'yes' more often!

Persuading others of the merits of our ideas, aims and plans is a life skill and being better at it would benefit most of us. When you start to look for examples of 'pitching' and 'proposals' you will find them in the most unexpected contexts. For example, the opening lines of any book are essentially a sales pitch. The potential reader has a short attention span, plenty of book choice and many other calls on his or her time. You don't have to be a trained salesperson to find yourself responsible for winning business or for presenting a business case for additional resources. Nor do you need to be an expert in marketing communication to be challenged to produce proposals that inform and persuade. Anyone who takes responsibility for building business – from TV producers and consultants to landscape gardeners and departmental heads – has a need for effective and convincing business communication. In today's competitive marketplace pitches, proposals and presentations are often the only doorway to additional resources and new, or even repeat, customers.

Your purpose in any pitch, proposal or presentation is to develop business communication that differentiates you from the competitors – to produce and deliver a compelling argument. Today's business clients have changed – they have the advantages of operating in a *buyer's market* – a market in which supply exceeds demand, resulting in the buyer having choice and being able to drive the selection agenda. The timing, environment and format of how competitive offers are to be assessed and judged is in the customer's hands.

Given such constraints, presenting with impact can prove challenging but your organisation's success depends on how well you can manage the process.

Pitches, proposals and presentations

Pitches, proposals and presentations exist in many variations and are used in a wide range of business contexts. For the purposes of this book I have differentiated between them in the following way.

- **Pitches** – a pitch is a face-to-face selling activity. It could involve selling an idea or product, or the capability of your organisation to tackle a specific project.
- **Presentations** – these are also face-to-face meetings but without a strong selling focus. Often used as a forum to feed back findings from a project.
- **Proposals** – these are written documents, including tenders, that support or replace the pitch. They are intended to help win business.

In practice there are many hybrids of these so you will need to pick 'n' mix from the tips and advice provided according to how your organisation uses these techniques.

In most markets, both internal and external, the process of assessing competitive offers is based on some form of pitches, proposals and/or presentations.

Decisions are made not on the objective reality of which offer is the 'best' but on the more subjective perceptions of which *seems* to be best. Organisations and management teams may set out selection criteria but it is difficult *not* to be influenced by the confidence of a presenter or the quality and logic of a proposal.

In reality, perception is influenced by many things – from the personality of the presenter to the audience's sense of how well he or she understands and empathises with their needs.

Bridging the gap between developing a solution and delivering that solution to a customer depends on the effectiveness of your pitches, proposals and presentations.

Today it is simply not enough to have a product or service which is functionally better than those of your competitors, you must also have a competitive edge when it comes to presenting your products and services. It is simply not enough to design the best service, you must also develop the best pitch to ensure it is demonstrably the best.

Mistakes made in presenting your offering to the customer come with a high price tag – so to ensure that you maximise the return on investment in product development and service delivery, it is worth investing a little extra in converting potential customers into actual clients.

In the following pages we will answer the questions below.

- Who needs to get better at pitching?
- What would it mean to you if you could improve your current success rates?
- Why do we all possess skills in persuasive communication?
- What is a competitive advantage?
- Why, so often, can the pitch be considered 'the missing link'?
- Whose job is it to pitch?

The impact of improving your success rate

In case you are still not convinced of the potential benefits at stake, let me ask you to consider what even a small improvement in your pitching and presenting skills might mean.

Consider the professional services team who currently win 1 in 5 pitches. What would be the business impact if it could stretch its performance ratio to win 1 in 4? Not only would this generate a 20% business uplift, it would do so without additional marketing and sales costs – so both profit margins and total profit should improve. But that is not the end of the benefits. Improving success rates will also help to build greater confidence, and winning teams win more often ... so next year a 1 in 3 success rate may be a realistic goal. If you want to be a high-performing team, improving success rates can drive significant performance improvements.

For those working to persuade internal customers, the bottom-line benefits may be less obvious but they are still there. Rejected business cases reduce the resources available to you and de-motivate your team. Think back over the past year – how much more would you have in the budget if your business cases were successful just 10% more often? What could those extra resources have been used to deliver? But budget isn't the only benefit of improved pitching. If others say 'yes' to you more often then the perception and image of you and your team is likely to be more positive. Your contribution to any debate will be valued more highly.

There is a lot at stake. Take a minute to think through what a 10% improvement in success rates would mean to you.

Calculate the business benefits

What is your current success rate?

Pitches [ ] Wins [ ]

What would a 10% improvement in performance be worth to you? £

What would a 20% improvement in performance be worth to you? £

You can use this analysis as an incentive for setting your own performance improvement objectives and measuring the effectiveness of the ideas in this book.

good ideas don't sell themselves

Persuasive communication – a life skill

Persuasive communication – the ability to convince others to your way of thinking – is a life skill. You started to learn the techniques as a child when trying to win the right to watch late-night TV or stay out an extra hour at a friend's party. At this early age you learned the importance of mutually profitable exchange – there had to be something in it for mum and dad, and that something had to be important to them. You probably offered persuasive benefits in the form of extra good behaviour or a tidy bedroom. At the same time you discovered the value of lobbying – speaking to your parents separately as you tried to influence their decision.

You probably still use the same skill set, perhaps to convince your children of the benefits of eating more fruit and vegetables or your friends that they will enjoy the latest film more than a night in the pub.

These pitches, proposals and presentations may be less formally planned and structured in the home and social environment but the skill set and techniques you use are exactly the same as those you need to develop if you want others to say 'yes' in the world of work. There are many scenarios and contexts where you and your team need to make pitches and presentations. The terminology may differ between organisations and sectors but the challenge and principles are common – in every case there will be an idea or proposal that needs agreement and support.

You may be:

- a business manager making a case to the Board for additional resources;
- a team leader trying to get agreement from colleagues for a new strategy;
- a manager of a professional services group having to pitch your ideas to a client;
- a business coordinator pulling together a tender document;
- a business partner needing to win an important new client.

Whatever your role, or the business context or language used, the persuasive task is the same and your success or failure matters. The best idea or product in the world will never be tested if you cannot convince your audience to give it a try.

Most organisations recognise the logic and importance of developing a better product but few recognise the benefit of improving staff persuasion skills or of pitching and presenting. Is *your* business losing out because its products and ideas are overlooked simply because they are not presented as convincingly as those of your competitors?

Building a better mouse trap – the basis of competitive advantage

Today's customers have choice, be they internal or external. There are many suppliers offering services and there is no shortage of projects that the bosses can allocate limited resources to. In the context of business today we are invariably in a buyer's market and this has serious implications. If the customer isn't satisfied with your offer or proposal you simply won't win the business. Even if your offer or idea really is the best, it will only be selected if the customer *perceives* it to be the best. How the proposal is pitched and presented is crucial in influencing perceptions.

It hasn't always been this way. In the past the balance of supply and demand in markets was different. Sellers' markets prevail when there is inadequate supply available. In such conditions the customer has little choice and must accept the available products. This period of business history is summed up well in the quote ascribed to Henry Ford, 'They can have any colour they want ... as long as it's black.'

Today's customers are not satisfied so easily. They are more knowledgeable and demanding, expecting firms to deliver quality and functionality as a minimum. But also expecting them to be able to differentiate their offer – in other words, as a seller you must be able to answer the question, 'Why should we choose you?'

This change in the balance of power in the marketplace has driven most organisations along the path of customer-centricity. More and more of them use marketing to help secure their offer – whether products or services, solutions or experiences – and ensure that it does indeed meet the customer's needs. Market research and innovation are used to ensure that our products are what the customer wants to buy. In other words, our offers have a *competitive advantage* – hopefully a compelling and sustainable one.

What is a competitive advantage?

A competitive advantage exists if your offer delivers more relevant benefits than the alternatives. This is why it is important that the script for any persuasive communication focuses on and highlights the benefits it represents – this is the decision-maker's agenda.

These benefits form the basis of customers' assessment of value for money, and their perception of the value that each alternative represents is the basis for decision making. If all the available alternatives represent the same value for money there is nothing to differentiate one from the others – in other words, no compelling reason why your offer should be chosen, no competitive advantage. In these circumstances the market would be commoditised and a rational customer chooses on the basis of price alone.

Value for money is controlled and delivered through the variables that influence the customer's buying behaviour – these are often referred to as the 'marketing mix' or the 'seven Ps'. Six of the Ps have the potential to add value and the divisor is price,

$$\frac{\text{Product, place, promotion, people, processes and physical evidence}}{\text{Price}}$$

The following table explains each of the marketing mix variables and gives an indication of how it might be used to add value to an external or internal customer.

Marketing mix element	*Value to external customer*	*Value to internal customer*
Product: the functionality of your offer (product or service) – in other words, what it does. For example, a car gets you from A to B.	May be in the form of additional functionality or superior performance, or perhaps a choice of functionality.	The proposal is the product – it may be a recommendation for change and it will offer the business benefits associated with moving the organisation from A to B.
Place: is about availability – when, where and how I can buy.	Over recent years, distribution has often been used as a differentiator: think of Direct Line or Amazon. Convenience, 24/7 availability and location are also sources of place benefit.	More difficult to envisage in an internal marketing offer but value can be changed by the timing of the proposal. Here you are considering the ease with which people can buy into your idea.
Promotion: the values associated with an organisation, product or team that influence its value to the customer – in other words, the brand. Promotion is also important because it impacts on perception – advertising and communication activities can highlight the benefits available and influence people's attitude to the organisation and product.	Branding differentiates products and services and in the process adds both tangible and intangible values to the mix. Products with certain associations and image can be more or less desirable to the user – this might be because of exclusivity or reliability. Your corporate reputation and brand can influence customer perceptions. The pitch, proposal or presentation is an important element in the promotion of a B2B offer and how you position yourself through this will impact on perceptions.	The sender, be that team or individual, has a personality and reputation that is the equivalent of the brand values. A reputation for innovation and good ideas will add value to your next proposal. Lobbying and presentations can be used to promote your business case and proposals.
People: those you have contact with are key to the value of any service delivered, be that a waiter or receptionist, security guard or consultant. Their technical and service skills can make or break the customer's satisfaction.	There are two aspects you need to consider: ◆ the composition of the team you are proposing to a client, their CVs and track record; ◆ those you are using to front your pitch – their empathy and confidence, credibility and influencing skills.	The reputation and track record of those involved with any project you propose will influence perceptions of how likely it is that it will be delivered. So publicising your own successes and improving your internal PR is a good strategy if you want to improve your credibility and success rate. Choosing the team to pitch and present also needs care – the most senior team member may not be the best person for this role.

Marketing mix element	*Value to external customer*	*Value to internal customer*
Processes: consistent delivery of a level of service depends as much on the processes that support front-line staff as it does on the customer service skills.	Can generate value in a number of ways. It may be that your methodology is tried and tested, and perhaps even endorsed by a third party – for example Investors in People or ISO 9001. Examples are your process for client management and key account handling, or your billing processes that perhaps help a client's cash flow. To understand how your processes can or could add value to the customer you must have an in-depth understanding of the customer's business.	This would be most likely to focus on the proposed methodology of your business case. The level of disruption and the proposals for managing the process to make it as smooth and painless to key stakeholders will be the basis for added value.
Physical evidence: refers to any tangible aspects of the offer – particularly important when dealing with intangible services. For example plans, handouts, staff uniforms, the physical environment and decor are all aspects of physical evidence. Think about all aspects of the tangible clues you are providing – *how would you feel about getting a quote from a landscape gardener who turned up in a Rolls Royce?*	As well as any tangible ingredients specified in your offer, the physical evidence of your pitch and proposal needs to be considered. The way that documentation is laid out and presented is a 'leave behind' that can change the audience's perceptions – though for many formal tenders the documentation is specified and standardised. You should consider whether samples or case studies can add credibility and impact. The chosen environment for a presentation (if it's under your control) matters and the dress and appearance of presenters makes an important impression.	The same rules apply. Consider the use of plans, samples and mock-ups to add impact to your proposals. The physical environment or format of a business case may be specified but make sure you use what is available as effectively as possible. Even when making a business case in presentation format, use handouts to summarise key benefits and reasons for supporting the proposal.

Marketing mix element	*Value to external customer*	*Value to internal customer*
Price: this seems straightforward enough but there are a number of ways that price itself can be used to add value or can be presented differently to change perception. Price includes actual price, cost of ownership and payment terms. It can be presented in terms of price per day or net of VAT to change perceptions.	This is the cost of ownership. The decision to buy or not depends on the *opportunity cost* – 'If I buy this, I can't buy something else, so I have lost the opportunity of the benefits that alternative purchase would have generated.' Customers buy the combination of goods that give them maximum benefit per £ of their income. Note that no one buys on price alone. If a customer tells you that your offer is too expensive they mean it doesn't offer as good value for money as another product – the opportunity cost is too high.	There may not be a price tag in the same way as on an external proposal, but that does not mean there is no cost! Again the concept of *opportunity cost* is important – 'If I resource your proposal I cannot enjoy the benefits offered by an alternative business case.' It is also important to recognise and take account of all cost aspects. The price of your proposal is change, and that always involves cost for someone – stress or hassle, uncertainty or loss of confidence. The benefits of your proposal must be greater than its inherent costs.

These P factors are important in the pitching processes because they represent the ingredients of your offer and a means of influencing perception. While each element of the mix communicates to the audience, it is the *combination* of elements that creates the whole offer – a range of benefits that the customer divides into three categories:

- **core benefits** – the main problem the product or service is addressing;
- **expected benefits** – a range of additional benefits offered by all the key competitors and which the customer has come to expect;
- **augmented benefits** – these are the differentiators and used to be referred to as the USP – unique selling proposition. Customers choose between competing suppliers based on these differences.

To be shortlisted as a possible contender for a contract, your organisation must offer all the core and expected benefits. These represent the specification, or minimum buying criteria. A supplier who fails to deliver these will not be considered by the customer so they are sometimes referred to as *cull criteria* – literally the criteria used to decide who is to be considered and who is not. A competitive advantage depends on you having *that something* in your offer that you do better than the competition, or that they do not offer.

Buying a house

You will have used your own cull criteria if you have bought or rented a home. You start with the list of core and expected requirements – three bedrooms, 15 minutes walk from the station, south-facing garden and good schools in the area. When the list of potential properties comes from the estate agent, you use your list to cull the non-starters from those you want to view.

If your team is not getting to the shortlist for work, you need to review the core and expected benefits you are offering. Perhaps customers expect ISO 9001 or that training is included in the price. You need to put this right before you pitch.

If everyone in the market offers the same core and expected benefits and nothing else then you have a commoditised market where the customer buys on price and the business goes to the lowest-priced competitor.

If you feel that your market has become commoditised and only price matters to the customer, then try to avoid competing on price. It tends to lead to price wars and eroded margins that leave you working harder rather than smarter. Instead, look at the customers you are pitching for and try to identify something that will differentiate you from the competition – something that the customer will really value. If you are lucky, you will find something which is relatively cheap to you but very valuable to clients. This will give them a reason to choose you.

Cheap and valuable

A 'cheap for you' and 'valuable to the client' scenario requires an open mind and innovative attitude, as can be seen from these examples.

- A builder's yard recognised that it had queues of customers first thing in the morning as builders collected materials for the day's job. So, it provided a service that allowed the builders to phone through their orders the night before. This saved the builders time and money and encouraged them to stay loyal to the business.
- In Detroit a motor insurance provider has distributed loss adjusters, in cars, around the city. A call from a motorist involved in an accident now results in a kerbside service, where a cheque for damages can be signed over or other assistance given as needed. This produced very satisfied clients and significantly reduced backroom operations and costs.

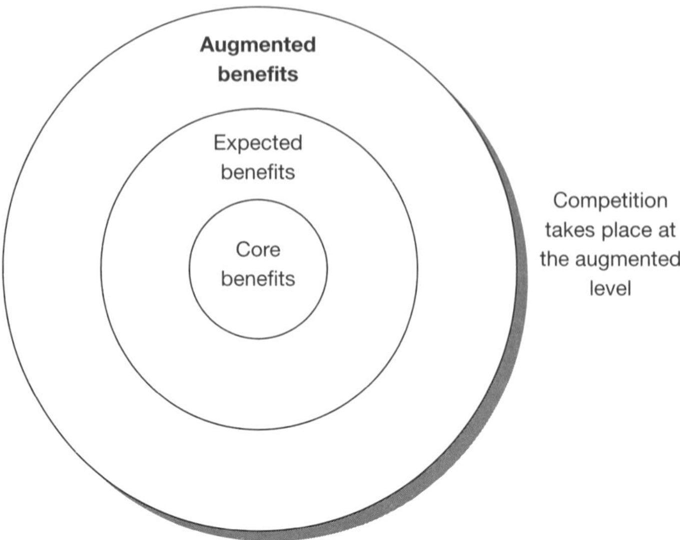

These three levels of benefit create what is known as the *total product concept* – the offer.

If you have developed an idea or offer that qualifies at all three benefit levels you have a winning idea.

If your team is not winning business, or not even reaching the shortlist, there are two possible reasons:

- **Your offer is not as effectively differentiated as that of the competition – they are offering something the customer values more highly.**
- **You have failed to pitch or present your proposal as convincingly as the competition. Remember, customers judge on the basis of their perceptions – a badly done pitch can damage even the best product or offer.**

You will need to do some research with customers you failed to win if you want to identify and tackle the cause of your poor performance. This is as important to internal business cases as it is to external ones. If the management team is faced with four proposals from business teams each promising the same return on investment and with similar risk profiles, the decision as to which to use will be made on other benefits valued by the business. Perhaps one provides the chance to build new staff skills and competencies, or increases the customer base.

Have you given them a reason to say 'yes'?

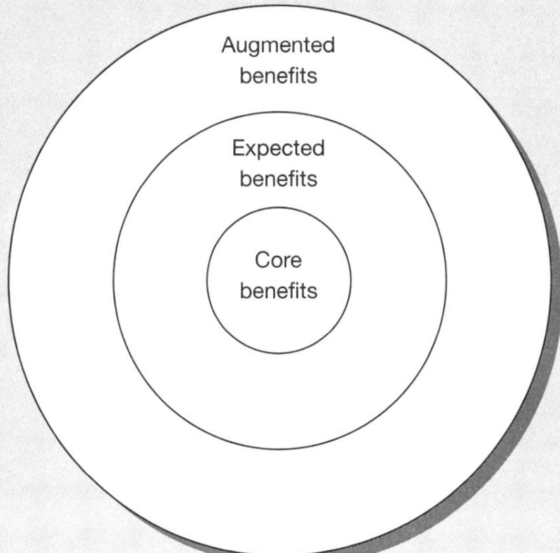

Take a recent project or piece of business you were *unsuccessful* in winning.

- Did you know enough about the customer to identify the core and expected benefits? If not, you need to get much closer to customers if you expect to win their business. You need to do some research.
- Now, add the additional benefits you used to differentiate yourself from the competition. How do you know these weren't also offered by the competitors? How do you know they were things the customer values?
- Now take a long look at your business, its capabilities and competencies. Use the earlier table describing marketing mix to help identify benefits you could potentially develop and offer as a means of differentiation.

What is a sustainable advantage?

A sustainable advantage exists when the benefits that differentiate your offer from that of the competition cannot be easily copied. This is often related not to what you offer or do, but to how you do it – the personality of your organisation. This involves the brand values, your business approach/ethics and your relationship management. Think about the experience of doing business with you and your team – what makes it distinctive?

Reviewing your relationship management

- Think about a project or business initiative you have completed recently. How good was your relationship management?
- What did you do to keep the client or senior management team up to speed with progress?
- Since completion how have you reviewed the client's or the management team's satisfaction with what was done and achieved?
- What have you done to identify the next piece of work you can undertake for this customer?
- What percentage of your work this year has been with repeat clients – by volume and value?
- Is this figure rising or falling?

It is estimated to cost five times as much to win a new client than to retain an existing one. Too often, management focuses on the pitches and proposals needed to *win* business and pays too little attention to the actions that can help *build* and *retain* it. Remember also that regular and loyal clients are likely to become advocates for you and are likely to endorse you when you need them to help win other pitches.

If your relationship management processes are poor or patchy, treat this as a priority area for action – it will impact on the bottom line more quickly than anything else.

The pitch – the missing link

In most organisations, effort is focused on two activities:

- developing an attractive product or offer;
- servicing customers who buy that product or offer.

What seems to be missing is paying equal attention to presenting the offer when trying to attract the customer in the first place. Clearly, having a winning offer or proposal is important but many teams spend so long developing a business case that they fail to allocate the necessary energy and commitment to the presentation process.

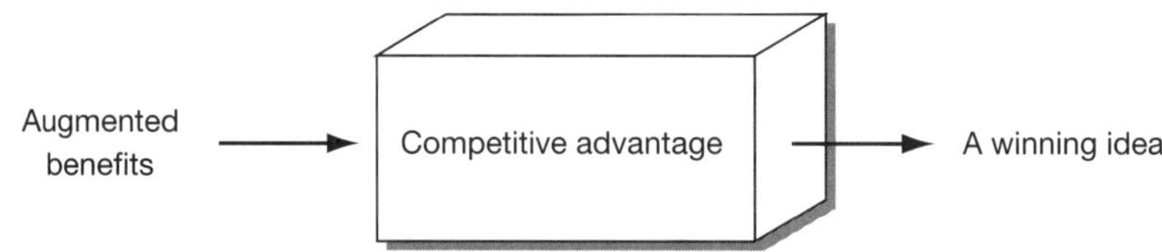

Instead:

- they hope the product's features will be enough to persuade the client;
- they convince themselves that the merits of the business case are self-evident;
- they tell themselves that the innovative proposal speaks for itself.

Unfortunately this is just wishful thinking. The best ideas and products are not necessarily those that get chosen. Perception is key in decision making and the way in which an idea is presented can strongly influence perception, and hence the choice of decision-makers.

An equal amount of attention is spent by organisations on improving customer service ensuring every contact or touch point with the customer is positive. As already seen, this emphasis on relationship building is essential. In markets where customers have a choice and where supply exceeds demand then winning new customers means taking business from someone else and overcoming all the barriers associated with this. In such circumstances there is an obvious logic to working hard to protect the client's lifetime value – this is the key to a profitable future.

So to be successful you need to:

- develop a product/offer that meets the customer's needs more exactly than the competition does (competitive advantage);
- work to retain and build a deep relationship with customers to maximise your business with them over their lifetime (sustainable advantage).

You won't be surprised to know that establishing and sustaining a competitive advantage and improving customer service are hot topics found at the top of most management agendas.

Perhaps you have noticed a missing link – you make a great offer and you are confident that you can deliver the product in a way that delights the customer, but you have taken the winning of the customer for granted.

Of equal importance, but less likely to be high on management's agenda, is the crucial topic of improving presentation and pitching skills. This key step in the process of winning and retaining customers is the subject of this book. In practice

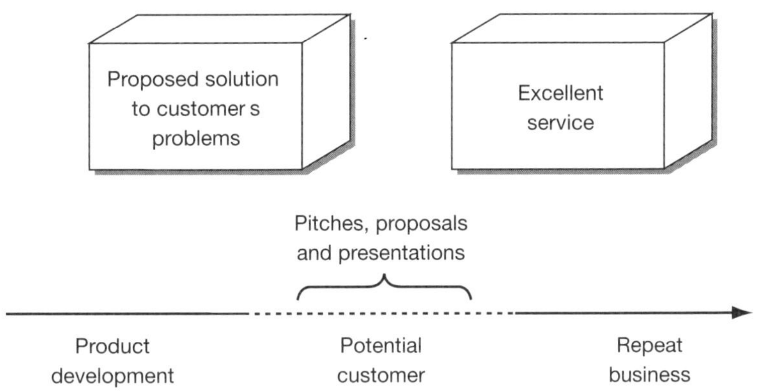

it is a relatively small part of the process but nonetheless a crucial one in persuading the customer that your solution to its problem is the best and that your delivery will be reliable.

When considering the problems and barriers to be overcome to improve success rates when pitching ideas, you must address the problem of determining who is responsible for this step in the building business process.

It's not my job

In practice, many of those responsible for presenting ideas and proposals would not consider themselves to be sales or marketing professionals. In the area of professional services, for example, it's the experts – be they architects or accountants, builders, gardeners or IT consultants – who present their plans directly to clients. Account management and business building is just a small part of their role – often one that is not much liked.

In thousands of small companies the partners and owners take the lion's share of sales building because there are not enough staff to designate a specialist salesperson, or if there is a high value-to-sales ratio not enough sales to justify a full-time post. Even those with dedicated sales teams often flounder when responding to tenders or delivering a formal sales pitch. Too often the salesperson tackles the process alone, without the direct support and involvement of the operational team whose skills the client is being asked to buy. If you focus on internal activities and making business cases, it is likely that you have never even considered the process as a sales activity.

In many organisations this is the root of their problems – the pitching of proposals is crucial to success but not high on any one person's agenda. Too often the wrong people are doing the wrong pitches, and the resources available to develop and deliver them are inadequate. Our approach is at best ad hoc, and at worst amateur, with few processes and systems in place to ensure consistency of approach and still fewer to ensure we learn from experience.

How effective are you?

To end this chapter, review the current roles, responsibilities and approaches to pitching and presenting in your organisation or team. Score yourself for each factor on a 0–5 scale where:

0 = never true
1 = once or twice
2 = sometimes true
3 = true about half the time
4 = true most of the time
5 = always true

You might also like to encourage your colleagues to do this activity to see how similar perceptions are across the team.

Factor	*Score*
We have and use a clear set of criteria to help decide which pitches, tenders and cases we should compete for.	
We monitor our success and failure rates to help improve our selection of prospects and opportunities.	
Those who take responsibility for pitches and presentations are the best people for the job.	
Those who deliver pitches and presentations treat it as a priority activity and allocate enough time to do the task professionally.	
Everyone in the business recognises the importance of pitches and will provide the support needed to help make pitching a success.	
We have access to the specialist skills needed – for example, editing skills for tender documents and desktop publishing skills for business cases.	
We are constantly looking for ways to improve the impact and effectiveness of our proposals and pitches.	
We have a framework and templates in place to ensure that our processes and approach to presentations are consistent and reflect our values.	
We have mechanisms in place to follow up pitches and presentations and to find out why we were successful or why we failed.	
We take time to debrief all pitches and presentations and learn from the successes and the failures.	
TOTAL	

Scores

33–50

You and your team take pitching and presenting very seriously, you allocate resources to it and strive to keep improving. Use your scores and the detailed factors to help identify areas for further improvement. Use the tips and activities in the rest of the book to become a consistently highly performing team who wins more often than not.

17–32

Your approach to pitches and proposals is haphazard and ad hoc. This implies a lack of leadership and strategy. The team needs to take time out to decide how to tackle this aspect of work. Consider identifying a small team of champions to review processes and procedures and make recommendations for improvements. The rest of the book will provide you with a structure and practical suggestions to help you plan for a more consistent and integrated approach.

0–16

The good news is there is plenty of room for improvement! This aspect of your work is a missing link and needs some serious attention and resource allocation. The danger is that you decide to make ad hoc improvements based on the ideas and tips in this book. Take time now to look *in detail* at the potential benefits a more serious approach to pitches and presentations might deliver. If that is convincing then make a business case for the resources needed to tackle the whole area as a priority project. Give yourself a specific timeframe – three months should be enough – during which you can develop a strategy and processes and begin to build the resources needed. The rest of this book will provide you with some of the blueprints and ideas to help.

spotting the pitfalls

The value of auditing

The difference between being an average or high performer in any context depends on an enthusiasm to improve. The starting point is being able to assess your strengths and weaknesses honestly and then having the motivation to tackle those aspects in need of improvement. At the end of the previous chapter you had the opportunity to review your current attitude to and processes for carrying out pitches and presentations. In this chapter you will audit your own skills in the area, as well as review some of the fundamental models and processes you need to understand to be a persuasive communicator.

This chapter answers the following questions.

- How can a simple model of communication help me to audit processes?
- Who are the key players in the buying process?
- What formats are there for delivering persuasive communication?
- Why is encoding your message so critical?
- How can noise be managed?
- What are the strengths and weaknesses of your current activities?

Throughout this chapter you will have the chance to review your skills and approach and assess your current strengths and weaknesses. Keep a note of these so you can complete your own audit at the end of the chapter.

A simple communication process

Any presentation or pitch is a communication activity. Helpfully, we can use a simple model of that communication as a diagnostic tool to audit your current approach and identify weaknesses and potential pitfalls. We will take each element of effective communication and look at what can go wrong during a sales pitch or proposal.

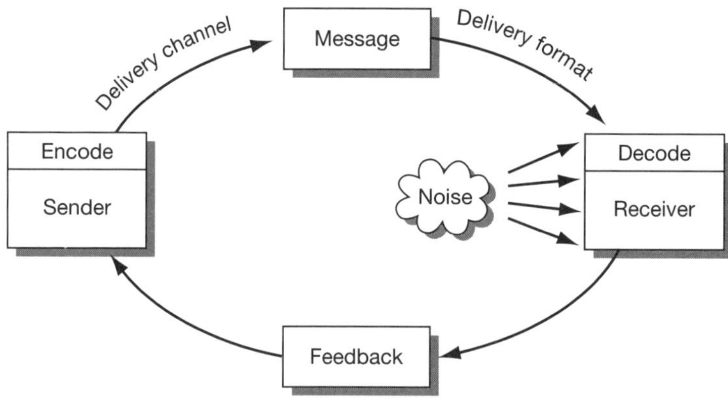

On the face of it, this looks a simple enough process. For any communication to be effective there must be a sender, a receiver, a suitably encoded message and an appropriate channel of communication. Feedback from the receiver will help the sender to judge the success of the communication, including how well the sender's message has been heard above the general 'noise' level.

What might surprise you is how many things can go wrong with this basic process. Once you are aware of the potential pitfalls and problems, you will be in a better position to take steps to avoid them.

You might like to reflect on your own experiences of failed communication at work and at home and create a list of potential problems before you read on.

The sender

Messages – proposals, tenders or business cases – have a source, the *sender*. The *receiver's* perception of that source will influence how that message is viewed. Awareness of your current reputation and image with different receivers is important to winning business.

Fundamental to this perception is your credibility. Why should the receiver pay any attention to your views and recommendations? Never take your credibility for granted.

- Try to find out how you and your organisation are viewed. Internal colleagues and past clients are likely to use your track record as a basis of assessment. If your last project was delivered late and over budget this will be in their minds and is a barrier to your success. It may be better to address this issue directly using information about what has been done to put things right. Even if both parties ignore the issue this does not mean that it won't influence decision making. At the same time, if your past record is strong then highlight this with reminders of your reliability or accuracy.
- Presentations in the context of a business environment need to build on and promote the values associated with the organisation's or team's brand values. In this way you are also leveraging the past investment in credibility building. Make sure your materials are branded (unless expressly forbidden) as a reminder of who this message is from.
- Take the time to brainstorm a list of the clues *you* would look for if asked to assess the credibility of an unknown supplier in your sector. Now think about your last presentation – how many of these were provided for the audience?

There are no formulaic answers to the question, 'How do we build credibility?' but the examples below might give you ideas and insight that will be useful in your own business context.

- In some contexts the dress of the sender adds credibility. Think of how doctors and police use uniforms to add authority to their messages. In your environment the way in which your team presents itself, or how a written case is physically presented, can give the receiver clues about values such as professionalism and attention to detail.

- The job titles and seniority of a team making a pitch can give receivers an insight into how seriously their business or support is wanted. In some cultures, particularly in parts of the Far East, staff seniority is judged by the quality of the hotel they are staying in. Sending junior staff to pitch would be an insult to the potential client company.
- Track records are a very useful source of evidence in seeking to prove credibility. Who else have you worked for and what results have you generated with past proposals? A receiver needs to feel that such references are relevant, perhaps in terms of sector or budget, the type of problem or the constraints of the project. Many organisations have a single list of past patrons and clients which is delivered with little commentary and the same list is used to support every proposal. This lack of customisation means that the audience is less likely to engage with or relate to the endorsements being provided.

- **Make a point of building a portfolio of case studies and past projects. This is just as important for an internal team as for one targeting external clients.**
- **Categorise these by budget/sector/outcome/approach, etc. so that you can easily select relevant examples to support potential new business.**
- **In circumstances in which you have no direct experience, borrow cases from elsewhere to illustrate the outcomes you might expect. For example the HR team proposing an incentive-based reward scheme for the call centre may have no direct experience to draw on but can provide evidence from similar projects.**
- **Where appropriate use external bodies to provide an objective view of your credibility. This could be membership of a trade association having a quality award like ISO 9001 or Investors in People.**

The receiver

It is crucial to understand who will be on the receiving end of your proposal. This information is not always easy to find but research and understanding is essential if you want to tailor your messages to the different members of your audience. Marketers use the term DMU – decision-making unit – to describe the collection of individuals that any seller might face. Each person in the DMU has his or her own agenda that the proposal must address if it is to be successful. It is therefore important to recognise the various roles, who fills each of them and what their likely interests are.

Roles in the buying process

There are many variations in the roles in a buying unit but they can be characterised broadly as follows.

- **The buyer** – the person acting as buyer has authority to negotiate and sign a contract. Buyers are generally concerned with processes associated with fulfilling the contract – they want 'an easy life' so need to be reassured that the expectations raised in the pitch will be satisfied after purchase.

- **The gatekeeper** – often an administrative role that controls contact with and access to other members of the decision-making team.
- **The adviser** – in many scenarios advice is given by third parties, sometimes referred to as 'coaches'. Advisers could be consultants or external parties recommending a supplier or an approach. They are concerned with retaining credibility with the company. They want to be confident that their advice will prove to have been good. They may be protective of their prior claim to a relationship with the client, and may be wary of a supplier who they fear might cut them out of ongoing involvement.
- **The financier** – in most scenarios there is a financial element and someone acts in the role of the economic buyer. Financiers are concerned with the financial aspects of your proposal – costs versus benefits, cost of ownership, and terms and conditions associated with your proposal. They need to be convinced about value for money.
- **The user** – in a first purchase, users are often not involved in the decision but their views have weight when there is a repeat purchase.
- **The decision maker** – in reality this is often the most difficult role to research. It could be the Board, a management team or the owners. It will often involve more than one person and internal politics and agendas can influence how the group responds to your pitch. Finding out who will make the decision is one thing; identifying who has the influence and authority can be something else!

Identifying your DMU

Trying to relate this model of the decision-making unit to the reality of your own experience may take a little time. To get you familiar with the terminology and concepts, try to complete the grid (overleaf) for a recent pitch or business case. If you can identify the business titles and work roles of those undertaking the various decision-making roles you will find it easier to relate to the grid.

Once you have completed the grid, review the pitch or business case you made and answer the following questions.

- How well do you know your DMU? Do you know who will be involved and their likely needs/agenda? Where are the gaps and how, with the benefit of hindsight, might you fill them?
- To what extent do you respond to these different needs and agendas?
- To what extent do you spell out benefits of your offer or proposal in terms that are relevant/meaningful to this mixed audience.

▶

Decision-making role	*Business title/role*	*Name*	*Agenda/interests*
Buyer			
Gatekeeper			
Adviser			
Financier			
User			
Decision-maker			

In Chapter 4 we will be revisiting the DMU when we look at techniques for getting to know the client.

In our analysis of the receiver so far, we have looked at the different roles of people who can and do influence the decision-making process. Before you leave your analysis of the receiver it is worth putting all these individuals 'back together' in their group or organisation. Take a step back and summarise what you know about the team or grouping that your receiver represents.

Factors that govern methods of communication

If it is a company, what is its strategy and culture? What are the key issues shaping its agenda? The context for your communications would be very different if faced with these two organisations.

Company A

Relatively new company with a young team, aggressive growth targets and impressive track record to date. It values innovation and ethical aspects of business highly.

Company B

Targets down-market segments of its own market, long established with a steady but uninspired growth rate and track record. Strategy focused on cost control and selective development of 'me too' offers.

In the case of presenting a business case, how might your approach change if you were faced with the following profiles?

Team X

This management team has worked together for a number of years. Members have a reputation for being sticklers for detail and are against taking risks in their decision making. They value reputation and loyalty and will need to be reassured that you can live up to your promises.

Team Y

A project team put together from across the business. Members tend to be high achievers who are enthusiastic about the opportunity to run this project. They care about outputs and want to know that you will fit in with the team.

The different characteristics make a difference to style and approach, don't they? It's not so much that the message changes but the parts you highlight and the language you use should reflect the receiver's context.

Made-to-measure or off-the-shelf?

Here is another question for you to consider. To what extent do your presentations reflect different receiver profiles? Do you customise or standardise your approach?

Delivery format

Once you understand your receiver in some detail, you can decide on the appropriate channel of communication or delivery format. However, in many business scenarios you will find this is specified by the client and you will have little influence on how your proposal is to be delivered. It is important that you establish and take account of any such constraints before putting your proposal together because the format will influence the style and approach you adopt.

The business sector and culture of the client organisation will determine the procedures adopted for evaluating possible suppliers or considering business cases.

Formats

The most formal and constraining format is the *tender*. Tendering is often used by public sector organisations and in large building and construction projects. A specification or brief will be provided to all potential suppliers along with a set of standard documentation containing set questions that must be completed and asking for supporting evidence that must be provided. Tenders can be very large documents and allow limited scope for creativity in terms of presentation, although the language and structure of answers to set questions can still have an impact on readers. The tendering process is designed to reduce subjectivity and bias in the buying decision process. The intention is to create a level playing field for those competing so that contracts are awarded on the basis of objective performance criteria.

Tenders are often employed to shortlist possible suppliers, and successful firms may still be expected to make face-to-face presentations.

Do not underestimate the work involved in tenders. Make certain you meet all the minimum requirements – quality standards, trading history, etc. – before starting the process.

Proposals

Proposals are also usually in a written format and can come before or after a presentation or pitch. If produced *before* then the proposal is a more informal way for suppliers to introduce themselves to the client. The structure and style are the responsibility of the sender and the content normally focuses on:

- how you will approach the project;
- your credentials and track records.

First impressions can make a significant difference to getting on to the shortlist or not.

Avoid the temptation to develop an off-the-shelf 'corporate brochure' that fulfils this introduction purpose. One size is unlikely to fit all and the customisation of your experience and approach to reflect the client's sector and language will help demonstrate your relevance and empathy. In this case, the intention is to get shortlisted. Your focus will be to establish your credibility and credentials for the work. You should also demonstrate your intended process – *how* you would approach the job. Don't try to solve the problem too early in the selection process.

Keep this in mind . . . 'Why should they shortlist us?'

If a proposal is submitted *after* a presentation, it will be much more specific and provide details of how the project is to be managed or of the solution being recommended.

Proposals may be used in this way for repeat work being allocated to preferred or established providers – note how this changes the focus of purpose.

The training proposal

As a training provider I have a number of corporate clients to whom I deliver programmes regularly. The learning and development team typically generate a brief and ask me to propose a training or learning intervention which they present to the business managers concerned.

The intention is to present and sell the training solution, rather than my credibility as a training provider.

The timing for a proposal significantly impacts on the focus of its content and also on your objectives when putting it together.

- **Before** – the objective is to get shortlisted, therefore you must meet the client's core and expected needs and use your track record and processes or approach to establish why you are worth considering further.

Just as the purpose of a CV is to get the interview not the job, so this type of presentation is to get to the shortlist not the contract. Take care, therefore, not to put too much into your documents. You need the readers to want to *know more* about you, to encourage them to meet you.

For example, giving a shopping list of clients from the sector and the projects completed for them is likely to be boring and leaves little to the imagination. However, a statement such as, 'Over the past three years we have managed £200 000 worth of projects for dozens of firms in this sector, including projects for companies X and Y that delivered the following. . . .'

Now your receiver will be wondering who else you have worked for and what the outcomes were.

- **After** – the work is likely to have been won in principle but the client now wants the details of your proposed solution or approach. A proposal used in this way can become part of the contract so attention to the specifics and details are important, especially budgets and timetables. A proposal used at this stage in the process really will firm up the client's expectations so don't fall into the trap of overpromising at this stage.

The pitch

The pitch is a face-to-face meeting between prospective supplier and client in business-to-business (B2B) contexts. The format is often quite formal and it is used to decide from the shortlist of suppliers. Location, duration and the available facilities will normally be decided by the buyer. This is often done to ensure that all those being considered are treated equally. It is important to find out the rules of engagement and the facilities available before you begin to develop the content or you may end up with too much to say and without the technology needed to say it.

Pitching for work in sectors such as advertising and research will involve your response to a detailed brief. The client is interested not just in who you are and how you work but in your solution to a specific problem or project. The quality and creativity of your solution and approach will be central to the success of your pitch. In sectors where pitching involves a response to a brief as part of the selection process, you need to take care to evaluate the opportunities to pitch (see Chapter 3).

The work involved on pitches in these scenarios can be significant and access to the client for additional information and data is often limited. In some sectors it is custom and practice to pay suppliers a fixed fee to mitigate some of the costs involved in pitching for the work, but even so this is unlikely to be a profitable use of resources if you always come second!

As with proposals, the pitch can be employed at different phases in the decision-making process. In consumer markets the architect or landscape gardener may have presented their credentials to win the opportunity to pitch, in the sense of responding to the specifics of the brief. It depends on the nature of the business as to whether the pitch is then seen as the first piece of work or as a final step in the decision-making process. Certainly, these professionals would expect to earn a fee for their designs but their goal may be to win the work of fulfilling the project and implementing the plans. Certainly, the client is likely to have the opportunity to reject the solution presented at this stage.

The presentation

The presentation is another face-to-face format for buyers and sellers and it can also be used at different stages in the decision process.

- To win the work or the right to present/pitch proposals – in this case, the focus will be on credentials and process. There may have been a brief of sorts but you will present how you would tackle it rather than a solution to it.
- Once a contract is awarded, the supplier may need to present its proposals for tackling the project. Unlike a pitch there is limited selling of ideas in this context. It's more likely to be a collaborative problem-solving opportunity.
- After a piece of work or project is completed the supplier may need to present findings and further recommendations to the client. Used in this way the presentation is both part of the original service and also a crucial point in the client/supplier relationship. There is often an opportunity to pitch for further work, and without doubt the level of client satisfaction and supplier credibility will be influenced by the way the presentation is managed.

The business case

The formats for presenting your message internally may have different titles but they mirror those described above. Once more it is the corporate culture that will determine the custom and practice of how business cases are made and presented at different levels in the organisation.

The thing to remember about making your case is that, whatever the format, the purpose is to assess the feasibility of the business case proposed – what will it cost and what benefit will it generate over what time frame and at what risk?

Competition won't come from others offering to do the same as you but from teams with an alternative use for the organisation's scarce resources. It is likely, therefore, that even if you are asked to present your business case, in reality you should be pitching it. Don't make the mistake of leaving out the sales element in your message – in other words, you must emphasise not just what you are proposing but why.

Understand the decision-making process

We have already identified the players in the decision-making unit. When thinking about the formats to use you also need to have a detailed understanding of the client's **decision-making process.**

- How does it short list potential suppliers?
- How does it decide between those on the shortlist?
- How does the successful company present its proposals?
- Are presentations needed at a later stage in the process?
- How is repeat work allocated?

Defining your decision-making process

- Can you answer these questions in your business? Note that your answers might differ between the different segments of your market where different strategies for pitching, proposals and presentations may be adopted.
- Choose a specific scenario and list the sequence in which the various formats – tender/presentation/proposal – could be employed.

Even if you are not required to do so, you can add impact by combining written and verbal formats so the presentation is supported by a written proposal, or the written business case is reinforced by a presentation to the Board. Often the written documentation can act as physical evidence reminding the client of you long after the presentation or pitch is over. You might like to consider whether you could add more impact by using formats in combination.

The message

Once you know the format and understand the audience you can get to work on the message – both its content and style. Written communication and verbal presentations differ and need to be developed differently. In later chapters we will be considering in detail how best to structure and deliver your messages in these various formats.

Those who are good at the written word are not necessarily the best at putting the script together for a presentation. Check out the skills of your team and identify who is best at what. Editing and proofreading skills are essential for tenders and written formats, whereas PowerPoint skills will help with presentations. If any of these core skills are missing in your team then take steps to fill the gap:

- **provide training and development for team members;**
- **next time you recruit add any missing skill sets to the job profile;**
- **identify third party supports – freelancers and external agencies will often be able to provide the skills you need.**

Knowing where you are in the decision-making process will help you set clear objectives for your message and this will inform the content.

Mind the language barrier
In the majority of cases, the supplier is a specialist or expert – at least more so than the client. It is therefore very easy to fall into the jargon trap. Using the correct terminology may provide evidence of your expertise but it tells the client that this will be an unequal relationship. Use everyday words if you can or, if necessary, explain technical jargon and terminology (but take care not to sound condescending).

- **try to provide clients with a page of key terms they may come across;**
- **ask a non-expert to review your proposals and presentations to check for jargon.**

The use of words and images to convey your meaning is known as *encoding* and the acid test of how effectively you have done this is how well/accurately your audience decodes the message.

Written formats are easier to police. They can be reviewed and checked, but face-to-face meetings bring other dimensions into play, such as body language, which can influence the receiver's perception.

Jargon free or not?
How well do you score when it comes to jargon? Take a look at several past proposals and presentations before you make your judgement. Count the jargon words and technical terms.

Noise and feedback

We are left with just two elements in our simple communication model.

Noise

Noise is a fact of life. It is the term used to cover the range of distractions that can prevent a person receiving and understanding your message clearly. The first, and perhaps most obvious, of these is the competitors' messages. You are in essence saying choose us, we are best; while the competition is shouting, **'No, they aren't – we are!'** Not surprisingly, the receiver can end up confused about who said what. Individuality and some creativity can help the receiver to retain your message and remember that it was you who said it. Coping with and planning for competitive noise is a key part of building your proposal or presentation.

When developing your offer you asked, 'Why should they choose us?' When developing your presentation ask yourself, 'Why should they remember us?'

Other types of noise can be less predictable and harder to manage. Environmental noise is associated with the location of your presentation or pitch, which you may not be able to influence. However, careful preparation should ensure that your speaker can be heard clearly and that other distractions are kept to a minimum.

Feedback

Feedback is essential if your presentations and proposals are to improve. Feedback comes directly in the form of successes and rejections, and these are metrics that need to be compiled and monitored.

However, qualitative as well as quantitative forms of feedback can be useful.

- Listen to the questions asked after a presentation. Has the questioner misunderstood or failed to hear something covered in the presentation? If so, what can you do to improve on this and stop it being a problem in the future? Next time you may not be lucky enough for someone to give you a second chance by asking for clarification.
- Talk to clients you have pitched to – both the successes and failures. Ask for detailed feedback on what worked and what you could do better. Make it clear that you are *not* asking them to justify their decision, rather to help you meet client needs more successfully.

Completing an audit

As you work on through this book we will revisit these key elements of the communication process and use them to help to structure our approach to generate better propositions, proposals and pitches. Throughout this chapter you have had the chance to consider your own strengths and weaknesses. Analysis is only the starting point – improvement is the result of actions. To help you record and organise your analysis, try using a sorting grid like the one overleaf.

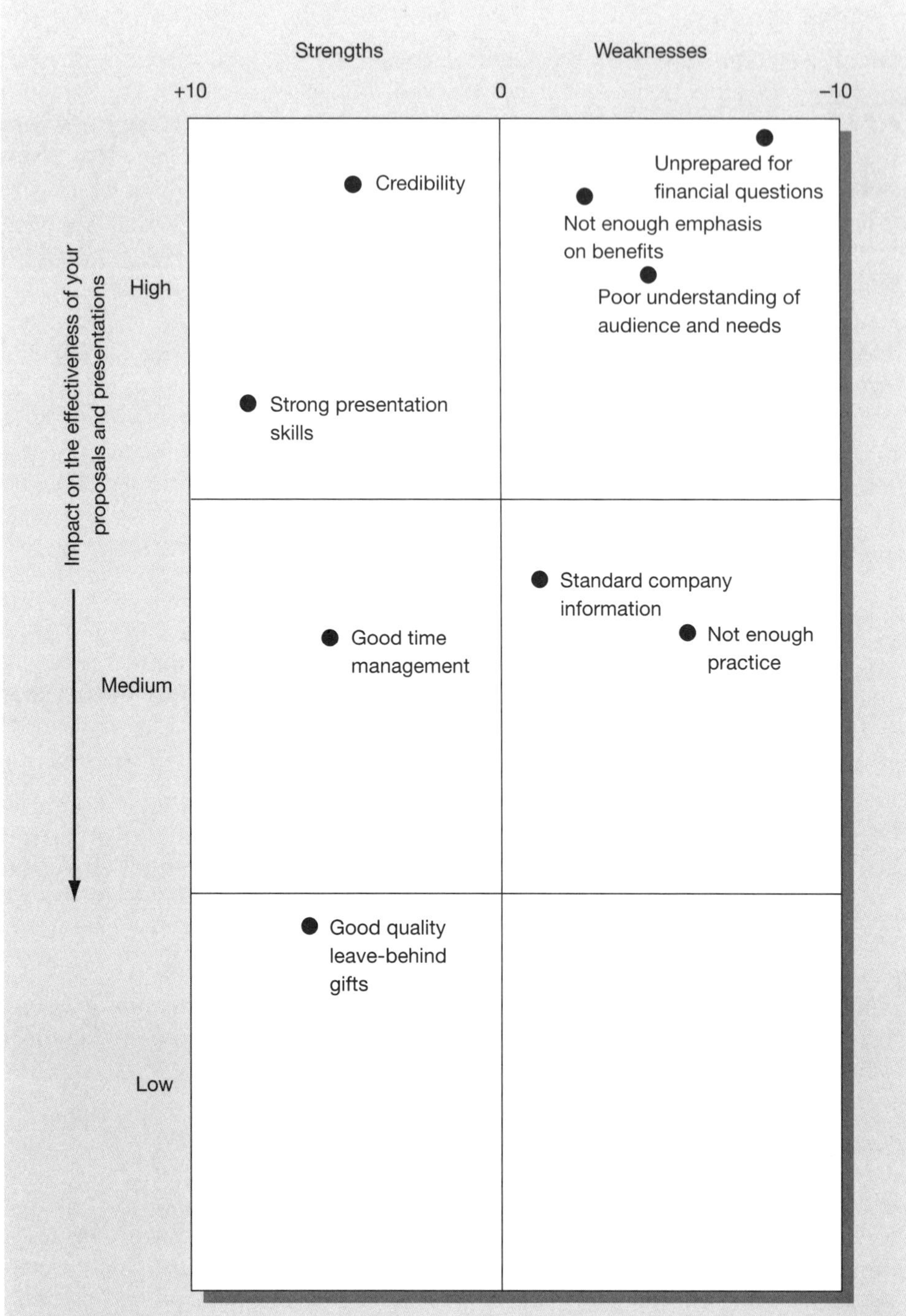

Top left are your strengths – build on them. Top right are the factors crucial to success – work on them. Bottom left isn't making an impact – so don't bother. A zero score indicates average performance – ok, but no better than others.

Use the grid below to record your own performance. The degree of strength or weakness will be a subjective judgement, but you can use your own experience to help you assess how important each element is in terms of its impact on the likely success of your presentation.

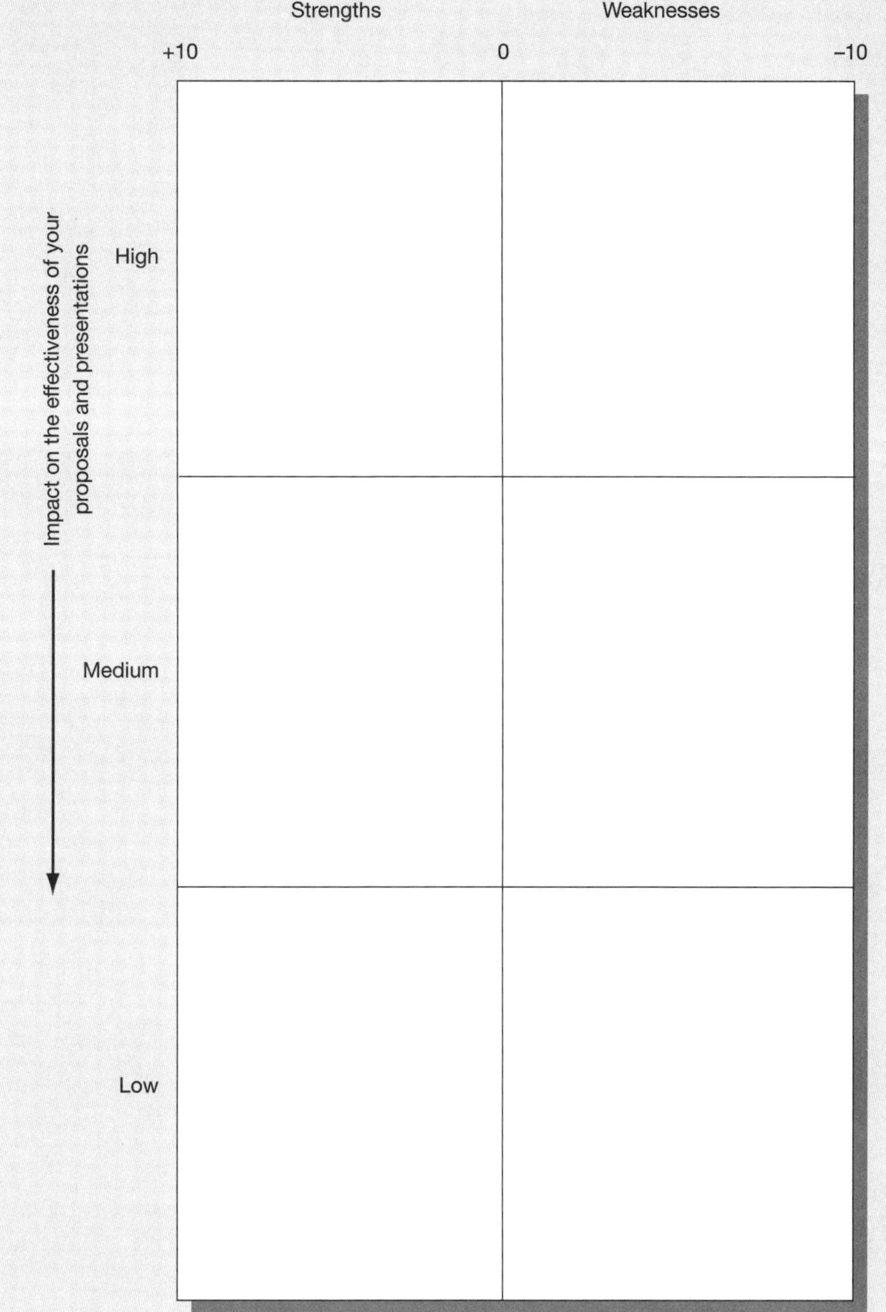

Remember that your weaknesses in the high impact cell (top right) need to be worked on as these are crucial to your success.

Troubleshooting

Whenever your communication efforts have failed you can revisit this simple communication model to help you diagnose the problem. It has to lie with one or more of these communication elements:

- poor perception of the sender;
- wrongly targeted receiver;
- inappropriate channel/format;
- the wrong message – in content or poorly encoded;
- too much noise;
- failure to decode effectively.

Use these headings to structure reviewing and debriefing sessions. This will help ensure that you have covered all the bases.

to pitch or not to pitch

Saying ‘no’ needs bravery

The facts and figures

Metrics matter

But who do we say ‘no’ to?

The challenge of profiling

Profiling the successes

Screening opportunities

Do we want the business?

Manage the volume

How to say ‘no’

Saying 'no' needs bravery

The resources needed to develop proposals, and to present and pitch effectively are not insignificant. They also need to be used carefully and selectively. It is better to do less but do a better job than to spread yourself too thin responding to every possible opportunity ineffectually.

Saying 'no' requires a certain level of bravery and confidence. We will look at establishing processes to help prioritise work opportunities and to screen requests before you respond to them.

This chapter answers the following questions.

- Have you got all the facts and figures?
- What metrics should you be keeping?
- How can analysis of basic data help you to improve the efficiency and effectiveness of your business building activities?
- How do you profile potential opportunities?
- How do you develop a set of criteria that will let you assess:
  - the attractiveness of an opportunity to your business?
  - the chances of you winning that business?
- How do you do less but win more?
- How do you say 'no'?

The facts and figures

Decision making depends on relevant and timely data and information. Information in the form of facts and figures which managers can interpret with insight to help them make better decisions – to get it right more often. There are two questions you need to address:

- What information is currently available to you in this area of your work?
- What information would help you to make better decisions?

Try keeping an information 'shopping list'. Whenever you find yourself making decisions but wishing you knew something ... add this to your list. Every month or so review your list to assess what information would be useful in the future. You can then sort this list to identify your information priorities.

	Easy to get	**Hard to get**
Need to know	This is your information priority	You need to plan to gather this information, but take positive steps to do so now
Nice to know	Use if it is readily available but it will have only marginal value	Ignore this

All managers need to be discerning users of information to avoid data overload while ensuring access to the information that will help them to build a competitive advantage.

The basic facts and figures that should be available to you are your success rates (see the flow chart below). This hierarchy creates a 'sales funnel' showing how many prospects you need on average to generate an extra piece of business.

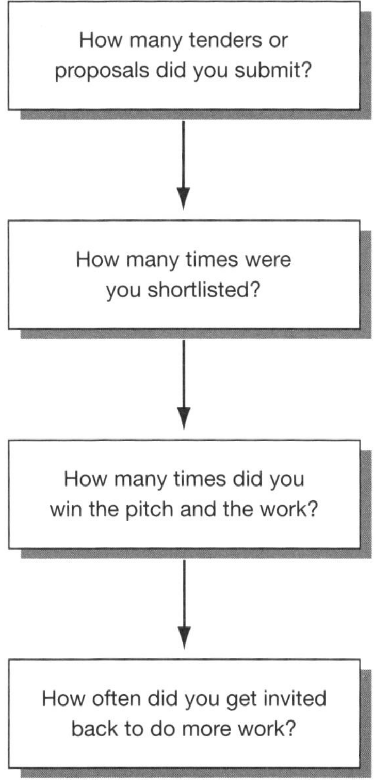
How many tenders or proposals did you submit?
How many times were you shortlisted?
How many times did you win the pitch and the work?
How often did you get invited back to do more work?

Figure it out

The scenario below provides a selection of the data that an organisation might have relating to its sales funnel.

Design-It is a ten-partner architect practice providing a range of services to both public and private sector clients. Last year the business submitted 75 tenders and proposals in order to get work. They were invited to pitch or present for 25 of these jobs and won five contracts worth a total of £1 million income to the business. Two-thirds of last year's income came from repeat clients, where there was no need to tender or pitch for the contract.

The partners have become concerned about their success rate in winning new business. The work involved causes stress and pressure for key middle managers. The company accountant has undertaken an activity-based costing project to help the partners assess the real cost of each activity. This is based on the actual resources used and their costs, *not* the lost-fee income from staff involved in presenting for new work.

▶

Activity	*Estimated cost of the activity*
Submitting a tender	£750
Developing and delivering a presentation (involving two staff)	£1000
Preparing and delivering a specific pitch	£1000
Producing a proposal to introduce the firm	£400

Using the information above, how would you answer the following questions for the partners of Design-It?

1 The cost of winning a new piece of business that involves a tender and a presentation is £1750.

True		False		Can't tell	

2 The company has a 5 : 25 success rate (20%) once they have been shortlisted. This is a good track record.

True		False		Can't tell	

3 Because tenders cost more to prepare than proposals, Design-It would be advised to focus on business that does not shortlist on the basis of tenders.

True		False		Can't tell	

4 If Design-It had improved its success rate at the first stage (tendering and proposing) from 1 : 3 to 1 : 2 it could have increased earnings this year by as much as £500 000.

True		False		Can't tell	

5 Last year the cost of fighting for new business was in excess of 10% of new revenue.

True		False		Can't tell	

You can compare your answers with those at the end of this chapter.

Metrics matter

Without detailed metrics you won't have the information you need to improve your performance or evaluate the potential of new business leads.

The Design-It example shows how simply keeping total figures may not give the insight you need. From the numbers you can calculate average conversion ratios, the average costs of winning one more contract and the average value of that work. These are, without doubt, useful. We can benchmark performance from one year to another to help set improvement targets. Because we have success indicators at different stages in the client's decision-making process, we can identify weaknesses and take steps to improve. This overall picture might generate a number of questions to help Design-It improve the efficiency and effectiveness of its sales activity.

1 What did Design-It do to generate 75 opportunities? What was the cost of this activity and can action be taken to increase awareness, and hence the potential client pool?

2 One in three tender proposals result in the company being shortlisted. Can this be benchmarked against competitors? Can team members talk to clients to find out why they succeed or failed at this first hurdle?

3 Once shortlisted the company's win ratio is 1 : 5. A 20% success rate from the shortlist may be disappointing (something is needed to benchmark this against to be sure) but if, on average, clients shortlist three companies at this stage, 20% is below a 1 : 3 success rate. Even if five companies are typically shortlisted, 20% is the share of business that might be expected so we must strive to outperform the market. Again further questioning of clients to help ascertain the reasons for success and failure might generate further insights.

A word of warning

When comparing yourself with others, take care. Different sales staff or organisations operate in different environments, so performance benchmarks are interesting but never tell the whole story.

Metrics in practice

A few years ago we were approached by an employee benefits firm who, among other services, managed pension funds for corporate clients. The firm was a relatively new market entrant but had grown rapidly and successfully. It had investigated the circumstances that triggered a review of pension fund arrangements in several companies and discovered that in each case the finance manager was key. A new financial manager appointment, or the organisation's need to make cost savings, could be the trigger for a review.

We were called in because the firm wasn't happy with its sales funnel performance:

- it was being invited to pitch more often and for bigger-sized clients than expected;
- it was failing to win an acceptable number of accounts.

These metrics were enough to prompt some further research. Taking a relatively small sample of organisations that reflected clients both won and not won, we undertook a series of qualitative interviews with key people in the decision-making unit, namely:

- the finance manager
- the HR manager
- the head of pension fund trustees.

What emerged very quickly was that, as suspected, the finance manager was the trigger for a review. The firm's promotional activity to the finance team of each company was resulting in the teams asking HR and the pension fund trustees to undertake a review. At the same time the teams had our client firm's name and details and suggested that it was invited to the '*beauty parade*' to see what it could offer. Thereafter, finance acted only as an adviser to the decision-making process, and indeed was not often involved in reviewing the shortlisted companies.

The key decision-makers were HR and the fund trustees. They were not dissatisfied with our client firm's offer but it was relatively unknown to them and didn't have the brand profile of the key competitors.

The solution was that the client firm developed communication and brand-building activities targeted at these other DMU members. By ensuring that it was not the mystery outsider in the competition for work meant it could improve its win rate.

This research, review and improved performance resulted from an analysis of the metrics.

But who do we say 'no' to?

What the figures tell us is the average cost of acquiring a new piece of business. That doesn't really help us to decide which opportunities are worth tendering for or which pitches deserve the creative input needed to do them justice.

Overall metrics do not allow us to differentiate between types of work, or indeed types of communication activity. If we revisit Design-It to see a more detailed level of the metrics it kept – the table above opposite – you can see the issues.

Even this simple level of analysis and record keeping gives considerable insight. If you were a senior partner in Design-It what conclusions would you draw and what further questions would you want answered?

You can see the strengths in the public sector and retail areas but the potential values are different. You need more than 1.5 retail contracts to match the worth of one public sector contract. Some questions worth asking are:

- Why are we bothering with the domestic market?
- What is our profile like in large corporates – do they have basic expectations we are not meeting?
- Are there more public sector opportunities we could be seeking, perhaps in Europe or in other areas of the public sector?
- Is our work as profitable in the public sector as in retail?

Client type	*Tenders*	*Proposals*	*Pitches*	*Presentations*	*Wins*	*Average order value*
Public sector	15			10	6	£125K
Large corporate	6	6	2	1	0	–
Retailer		30		10	3	£70K
Large domestic		18		2	1	£40K
Total	Opportunities 75		Shortlisted 25		10	£1000K

Even with these more detailed metrics you need to take care not to jump to conclusions. We could assume, for example, that all domestic work is worth £40K – but this is on the basis of one contract. Double check your assumptions – don't be surprised if your analysis leads to more questions.

Now that we have a more detailed breakdown of the Design-It activities we can look at the costs invested in developing business in each sector.

Client type	*£750 per tender*	*£400 per proposal*	*£1 500 per pitch*	*£1 000 per presentation*	*Total cost*
Public sector	£11 250			£10 000	£21 250
Large corporate	£4 500	£2 400	£3 000	£1 000	£10 900
Retail		£12 000		£10 000	£22 000
Large domestic		£7 200		£2 000	£9 200
Total cost	£15 750 on tendering	£21 600 on proposals	£3 000 on pitches	£23 000 on presentations	£63 350

Sector	*New business development costs*	*Additional revenue from business won*
Public sector	£21 250	£750 000
Large corporates	£10 900	£0
Retail	£22 000	£210 000
Large domestic	£9 200	£40 000
Totals	£63 350	£1 000 000

This level of analysis helps to prioritise new opportunities based on potential value and the likelihood of you winning the business. The return on business development is clearly highest in the public sector, even though tenders costs more than proposals.

We do not know the gross profitability for different types of work but if, for example, the margin on large domestic was 25%, we have invested £9200 to earn a contribution of £10 000. This is not simply a matter of mathematics, we should also consider the time and strain that the 18 proposals and two pitches/presentations represented, and of course the fee income those staff might have earned if doing something else.

The challenge of profiling

It is easy to develop illustrative examples, like Design-It, where the points are extreme and the learning obvious. Unfortunately, life is not always so straightforward and the first challenge is how to profile your activity so that the metrics reflect something meaningful. The second is what level of detail do you monitor at. Why, for example, did Design-It record its track record for retail business but *not* for NHS contracts within the public sector?

The key to successful segmentation of your new business opportunities is identifying groups or clusters of opportunities where the buying behaviour or need is similar. Competitive advantage can only be developed for a grouping who shares something in common. You don't know whether you aren't winning work from, for example, large corporates because your offer isn't good enough or because you have failed to present it effectively.

The answer to the profiling question will vary by business and by sector. The local builder might find that it is most useful to track opportunities by type of business:

- extensions
- loft conversions
- new build

- kitchens
- other.

The IT support services might decide that the use of an attitude to IT was more relevant:

- IT is mission critical;
- IT is a support function.

Those monitoring success in winning business cases from internal customers might monitor success based on who is being pitched to, the average value of the project or type of project.

As for the level of detail in your metrics, the greater the better, at least in the first instance. Clearly this needs to be at a practical level and so depends on the volume of activity you are trying to handle. Think about the cost/benefit of your analysis. If investing £10 000 in better measurement and analysis saves you £20 000 in wasted effort then it is probably worth it.

Let's visit Design-It one more time and look at an even more detailed analysis of its success area – the public sector. If it had broken its records down further the following picture would have emerged.

Contract	*Tenders*	*Pitches/presentations*	*Wins*
NHS-related contracts	7	5	5
Education-related contracts	3	2	2
Local authority contracts	5	3	0
Total	15	10	6

Take care not to jump to conclusions. There may be many reasons for differences in performance like this, but it does beg the question as to why your hit rate is so high in education-related projects and so low in local authority projects. Simply use your analysis to help build up your understanding of where you are doing well and where less well. Then let these insights influence the strategic decisions of whether or not to stop responding to certain categories of opportunity – or at least analyse your performance in more detail.

Also remember that you do not need to do this detailed analysis for ever. Design-It may have tracked its public sector activities and found no significant differences between the categories, in which case the higher level summary is fine.

Find out what metrics you have available and who is responsible for them.

If types of opportunity are broken down, assess how helpful you think the categorisation is.

If you don't break the opportunities down currently, what subgroupings might be used and what insight could that give?

Type of opportunity	*Activities to get shortlisted*	*Activities to win contract*	*Number of wins*	*Average value*
Totals				

Profiling the successes

There is an alternative way to gain the insight needed to start assessing just which opportunities are worth pursuing. It involves looking for common characteristics among your successes. This might lead you to any number of useful insights. For example:

- most successes are for a particular type of work;
- you win most when you compete by pitching rather than presenting;
- your success rate is highest when so-and-so leads the team;
- all your wins have occurred when you have personal recommendations and a champion in the client organisation.

Whatever the characteristics, be it value or service level needed, you can use this to help develop a list of screening criteria to assess new opportunities against.

Screening opportunities

If you are going to be selective about when to pitch and when not, you need to think about two dimensions:

- your likelihood of winning the work;
- whether the work is attractive to your organisation.

This requires you to generate two lists of the criteria or characteristics that influence these two dimensions. The first list relates to your likelihood of winning the work and is a reflection of your potential competitive advantage – do you have what the customers value and can you convince them of that? This list will be specific to each market, and indeed segment within a market, but for a typical business that offers a series of training programmes the list might include:

- the track record of training in the sector;
- a reference and recommendation from someone within the company;
- flexibility with regard to location;
- the ability to support training with improvement metrics;
- expertise in the required topic area;
- a persuasive presentation/pitch.

Try to limit your list of criteria to ten or fewer – to keep life simple.

Scoring

You can now assess the various opportunities to submit proposals on the basis of this list. You can use a simple tick, cross and ? scoring system to assess whether you can meet the client's criteria in these areas. For example, suppose there were two opportunities to weigh up, **A** and **B**.

- **A** involves a strategic planning programme in a sector I have a lot of experience in and where I have worked with the company before.
- **B** involves a customer care course in the retail sector where I have no contacts and no experience.

You could indicate your ability to meet the criteria as follows.

Criteria	*Opportunity A*	*Opportunity B*
Track record	✓	×
Reference	✓	×
Flexible location	✓	✓
Metrics	✓	✓
Expertise	✓	×
Persuasive pitch	✓	?
Score	6/6	2/6

You can use your own scoring system – mine had six criteria so I have simply added the ticks. The chances of winning are indicated by the number of ticks and can be used as an indicator as to whether or not to tender.

Chance of success	*Number of ticks*
High	5 or 6
Medium	3 or 4
Low	0, 1 or 2

In this example, I would not go in for opportunity B but instead focus efforts on A.

You can, if you want, be more sophisticated in your scoring by weighting the customer's buying criteria. In the examples below there are five identified criteria influencing customer choice and these are weighted to indicate the relative importance of each.

Criteria	*Weighting*
Track record in the sector	4
A team we like	2
Ability to deliver within three months	1
Qualified staff	1.5
Project management capabilities	1.5
Total	10

When the opportunities come in you can rate how well you can meet a customer's criteria on a scale of 0–5. A score of 3 indicates that you are as good but no better than the competition.

Criteria	*Weighting (0–10)*	*Rating for opportunity (0–5)*	*Total*	*Reason for the rating given*
Track record	4	4	16	Lots of experience and completed cases
Likeable team	2	4	8	Many references to confirm this
Delivery	1	2	2	We will need four months
Qualified staff	1.5	3	4.5	No better than the competition
Project management	1.5	5	7.5	Excellent skills, recognised as industry leader
Total			38/50	

Your rating is, of course, subjective though you should try to be as objective as possible. Indications of likely success using this system are given as follows.

Chances of success	*Score*
High	33–50
Medium	17–32
Low	0–16

What matters in this analysis is the assessment of how well you can deliver what the customer wants. It may care about your ethical record or quality standards. The customer's criteria will vary by sector or segment, or even by individual client. If you get a brief or tender document that specifies the decision criteria make sure to use it! Also, do your homework – what does its website or annual report say?

Do we want the business?

So far we have focused only on how likely it is that you will win the business. The next step is to confirm that it is business you would want if you were to win it. This involves assessing if it meets or contributes to your organisation's objectives.

Criteria	*Comment*
Revenue potential £1000 K	This criteria would help Design-It focus on higher average-value projects
High propensity for repeat business	Currently it has a 2:1 repeat/new business rate – it would not want to dilute this
Profit margin per job *x*%	Ensuring that the work meets profit targets is important

Whereas the specifics of the customer's buying criteria need to change to reflect its different needs and values, the company criteria can be established, shared by all decision-makers and used to ensure consistent decision making.

The process and scoring system are the same as those used before. The first step is to get your management team together and agree on the criteria that are characteristic of a good piece of new business. This could be profitability, potential for repeat business, or the impact on a skill or piece of equipment in limited supply. The list will reflect your organisation, its values and culture.

The Design-It list might look like this. Note that the more specific you are the easier it is to differentiate between opportunities.

Criteria	*Comment*
Demand for project management skills, 15 days or less	If Design-It is short of project management skills, projects that require little of them will be favoured
Competitive intensity (no more than four companies to be shortlisted).	This sort of criterion would be based on past experience
Risk	This could be financial risk, the risk of bad debt or the risk of failing to deliver satisfaction

Again, each opportunity can now be rated in terms of its ability to deliver what matters to the company. For Design-It, domestic contracts with low value, higher risks of non-payment and limited repeat business probably score badly.

The beauty of this approach is that you are free to decide on the criteria that matter to you. You might value opportunities that stretch staff skills, that don't involve staff in significant travel or whether or not you like the client. The choice is yours. But remember that garbage in will lead to garbage out, so what is in the list really does matter. Again, keep the number of criteria limited and if you use the weighting and rating approach to scoring, have the weighting done by one or two people – this avoids an averaging effect. It is the senior managers who must decide if average billing value is more or less important than a target profit margin.

This screening approach ensures that your assessment criteria are applied consistently and that you are not chasing work that will not deliver business benefits. You can pull the two dimensions of your analysis together in one grid – however you decided to score your opportunities.

	Opportunities attractive to our business			
Chances of us winning the business		Low	Medium	High
	High	Review and pitch selectively	Pitch	Pitch
	Medium	Don't pitch	Review and pitch selectively	Pitch
	Low	Don't pitch	Don't pitch	Review and pitch selectively

This matrix helps to formulate your response on an opportunity-by-opportunity basis. Those likely to deliver the business benefits you want, and where there is a medium/high level of success, are the opportunities you should focus on. These are win–win opportunities. Those which aren't attractive and offer limited chances of winning are a waste of time.

Those across the middle diagonal need review. Your criteria and rating will show why they or you aren't going to be satisfied – currently they are win–lose opportunities. Can you change anything to make them more attractive to you or vice versa? If not, think hard about the cost and benefit of going for these opportunities.

Get your team to identify and weight the criteria (so the total is 10) that make an opportunity attractive to you. Remember to have just one or two people do the weighting. Be prepared for some heated discussion – everyone has their own view of what an attractive contract looks like! Be as specific as you can to make rating easy.

Now take half a dozen recent opportunities and have the team rate each against your criteria (use the 0–5 scoring system). You should find that the approach allows you to differentiate between opportunities – which would you pitch for and which not?

- Assess the value of this approach and identify a process for using it. Make sure that all staff responsible for assessment are trained so that they know what they are doing and why.
- Monitor its impact on your business carefully using metrics. Average success rates should improve and cost of pitching, etc. should fall. If not then you need to review your criteria – are you sure you have understood the drivers of buyer behaviour?

This approach and methodology can also be successfully applied to deciding what type of work you want to target pro-actively.

A word of warning

Make sure that you review your criteria regularly – making them more specific if you get more insight into drivers of success or if they aren't supporting your business strategy.

Manage the volume

The important message from this chapter is that more opportunities are not necessarily a good thing – going for too many can spread your internal resources too thinly and a poor success rate can be demotivating for staff.

But there is a practical concern. Many companies, in particular smaller ones, are often worried that they won't have enough business going forward. There is a tendency to think of such opportunities as lottery tickets – the more the better.

Hopefully, having considered the costs involved, you are now more sympathetic to the notion of 'less is more'. But what if halving your tendering or pitching doesn't generate enough new business?

To reassure yourself you need to return to your metrics. One last visit to Design-It – imagine it has set itself a target of winning £1.25 million of new business next year. What does it need to do to achieve this?

Well, if Design-It focused only on public sector work it would need to win 10 contracts at an average value of £125K. On current performance it wins 60% of presentations, so next year it would need about 17 opportunities to present to win 10 contracts. In this sector it is shortlisted 2 out of 3 times so needs to generate about 25 tender opportunities. Obviously it would make sense to build in a contingency element, so it may target 26 or more tender opportunities. Design-It would need to appreciate that if these arose equally over the year it would need to be doing a tender every two weeks or so.

You can do a similar activity with the retail sector, changing the targets for each group such that in total you deliver the business objectives.

Control mechanisms should now be set up to monitor your own key metrics, such as tenders submitted per month, success rates and average job values. Over time you can review progress against your plan taking steps to tackle any problems.

How to say 'no'

One consequence of being selective means that you need to say 'no' to some potential customers. It's important that you do this in a way that doesn't close doors permanently – you may want to build a relationship with them in future.

Before you say 'no' take another look at the opportunity.

- **Is the client one you have a past relationship with or may want one with?**
- **Is this opportunity one that might help you to deliver a new strategy?**
- **Are there any other compelling political or stakeholder reasons why you should say 'yes' at this stage?**

Exactly how to say 'no' depends on the nature of the opportunity.

- A fairly anonymous request for you to tender can be responded to with a letter of thanks giving a reason for your refusal. If you might want to be considered in future make sure you say so.
- If you were asked to tender or pitch as a result of someone's recommendation, try to make contact to thank them for the endorsement and explain why you are not putting yourselves forward this time.
- You might consider developing an 'off the shelf' proposal that can be submitted in these scenarios. This would emphasise your processes and approach. You might even consider setting a fee for developing a specific proposal – using price to limit demand.

Whatever the situation, don't take opportunities for granted – acknowledge them, and perhaps recommend another supplier.

Remember that the world is a small place and that people move jobs and change roles – they can have long memories.

You should by now have a list of metrics to help measure your success and to analyse processes for deciding whether or not to pitch.

In the next chapter we will be looking at how to research the customer, either to help in the evaluation process or to inform your pitches and presentations.

Answers: Figure it out

1 This is a tricky question and indicates how you can mislead yourself with metrics. The costs *directly* associated with this piece of work are indeed £1750 and so this is true. However, for every successful project there are 4 that fail to generate work, and not 1 tender but 15.

(15 tenders generate 5 shortlist places and tenders, and 1 piece of work). Looked at this way, the more realistic cost per piece of new business would be £11 250 for tenders and £5000 for the pitches, a total investment of £17 250.

2 Ratios are very useful for monitoring all aspects of performance but you must be careful with them. A single ratio like this 1 : 5 success rate tells you nothing – to be of value you need something to benchmark it against. If you knew that two years ago the rate was 1 : 4, you would know performance was poorer or, if competitors won only 1 : 6 you are better at this step.

3 Unfortunately you can't tell. We do not know the difference in success rates or the value of tender-based contracts versus those which were shortlisted on the basis of proposals.

4 This is true – a 1 : 2 rate would change the sales funnel.

75	tenders or proposals
↓	
37.5	A 1 : 2 success rate would mean 37 or 38 presentations or pitches. If Design-It continued to win contracts from 20% of the pitches . . .
↓	
7 or 8 contracts	
↓	
£1.4m–1.6m	revenue from new business

When you look at these metrics it is easy to make the business case for increasing the resources for tackling this aspect of the work.

5 You cannot tell the total costs exactly because you don't know the mix of tenders/proposals, pitches/presentations. But 75 tenders/proposals cost between £400–£750 each, and 25 pitches or presentations cost about £1000 – a total cost of about £25 000. It is certainly a significant cost and improvements in the efficiency or effectiveness here would impact directly on the profitability of the business.

getting to know the market

Real customer focus

In today's competitive environments, business success depends on the ability to be customer centric and externally focused. This is not simply a matter of corporate packaging, wrapping your offer in 'have a nice day' customer service standards. Real customer focus means that the customer's needs and wants are central to every decision made and every presentation given. This client-focused concept is easy enough in theory but it can be quite challenging to put into practice. The first obstacle to overcome is the subject of this chapter – you have to get to know your customer. The second is that you must know your competitors as well as you know yourself.

This chapter answers the following questions.

- What do you need to know about your customers and their business?
- What sources of information are available?
- How can you research the competitors?
- What do you include in your 'information needed' checklist?
- How do you organise your information gathering?

The sector context

The information you need about your customers and its sources will be determined to a large extent by the sector and the context of your activities.

If you have a broad client base it will be more challenging to get to know customers and their needs than if you are focused on a specific part of the market and you are a preferred supplier with close and deep relationships.

Business to business (B2B)	*Business to customer (B2C)*	*Internal audience*
In many respects this is the hardest market to work in as you have to find out about the client company, who's who, its culture and strategy and also about its customers. What are the big challenges the company faces? What makes research a bit easier is that there is often a smaller number of clients and it is possible to get face-to-face contact and relationships with them.	The challenge here can be getting detailed information and insight about how a consumer market might be segmented and the different agendas of the decision-making unit. This can be particularly difficult for smaller organisations without big research budgets.	In many respects this should be the easiest to research. Finding out who's who should be straightforward enough. What is harder to assess is the relative power bases and different styles or cultures of teams and business functions.

The role of marketing

In many organisations those presenting and pitching for business will be able to call on the support of professional marketers. In these cases a significant amount of the research and analysis needed will have been done for you by them.

Marketers have different job titles in different organisations, they can vary in their roles significantly and indeed there is often confusion about what marketing is and is not.

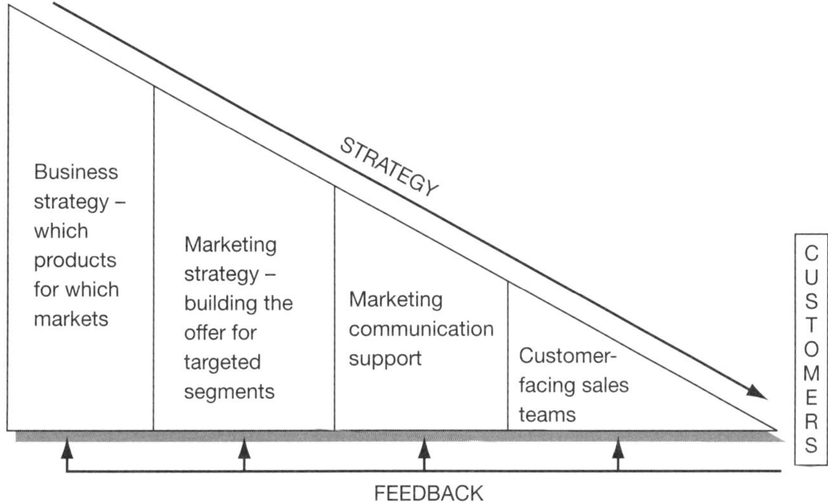

In a customer-focused organisation an iterative planning process looks like this:

Team	*Role*
Senior management or business planning team	Based on feedback from the market and front-line teams along with analysis and forecasts, decisions are made about which products and which markets the business will focus its resources on.
Strategic marketers	This is the role which is often missing in organisations that haven't truly understood how to become customer centric. This team takes each selected business strategy, segments the market, researches the customers and then orchestrates the development and positioning of the offer (core, expected and augmented benefits).

Team	*Role*
Marketing communications support	This is the role that many assume, wrongly, represents the whole role of marketing. This group should act as a bridge between sales or business-building staff and the rest of the organisation and its strategy. The group identifies, for each selected segment, who in the DMU need to be communicated to, and what message (benefits) should be promoted to whom. The group should be building integrated campaigns that help fill the sales funnel with qualified leads. It should also be treating client-facing teams as internal customers – working with them to develop appropriate and effective sales support materials, presentation aids, etc.
Customer-facing sales teams	This is the pitching and presentation team who should be using the strategy and support materials provided and applying them to the client prospects. Feedback about customer responses, needs and future plans should be an integral part of this role.

- **If you have professional marketers in your organisation, use them.**
- **If they are not delivering fit-for-purpose sales support materials or client profiles, tell them**
- **Marketers and sales teams need to work in partnership to be effective, so make the first move and set up a monthly dialogue with the team. Make sure your marketers go regularly with you to observe a pitch or presentation. If they don't understand the process they can't be useful in helping with the preparation.**

Build the big picture

Whatever the situation, try to start by building the big picture. Understand who's who in the market and what the drivers of change are.

Start by answering the question, 'What business are you in?' This is your mission statement and it is important that it is expressed in terms of the benefits you are offering the customer. Remember that customers – internal or external, business-to-business or business-to-customer – buy products and services, ideas or business cases because they have a problem or need. Making sure you understand what that need is and how your delivered benefits will satisfy it is a key first step in your customer-centric approach to the market.

The HR team that believes it is in the business of improving the working environment for staff will find it difficult to sell its business cases to the Board. If it recognises that it is in the business of improving productivity and performance *through* a better working environment then it is more likely to be addressing the needs of the Board and thus find a receptive audience.

Likewise, the builder simply offering a new extension misses the benefit – present it as extra living space and the benefits this can offer the family, and the proposal, will seem much more relevant.

Notice also that defining the business or offer in terms of the benefits will help you to identify your competitors better.

A market checklist

You may need to add to or modify the questions in this checklist to reflect the specifics of your markets, but they should help you get started.

- What benefits are being delivered in this market?
- How big, by volume and value, is the market?
- Is the market forecast to grow, remain stable or decline in volume and value terms over the next three years?
- What are the geographic boundaries for you in this market?
- What is the average annual customer value in this market?
- Who are the key competitors?
- What are the key drivers of change?

The drivers of change

The drivers of change come from the external environment and cannot be controlled by individual organisations. They could be regulation or legal changes, new technology or changes in spending power because of economic developments. Understanding these helps you to empathise with your potential clients – these items will be at the top of their agenda. To sell to other companies you have to know their business as well as your own. Evidence of your understanding and empathy with the challenges they face will be valued by your clients.

Competitors

Competitors are decided by your customer – the other firms invited to tender or pitch will consist of anyone who is offering the same benefits. Remember the core and expected benefits represent the cull criteria – the basis on which the customer decides who to consider as a supplier (see Chapter 1).

Do not be surprised to find that not all your competitors are in the same industry as you. The security company offering 24-hour on-site guards might find that the management team is also considering a security solution based on cameras and a surveillance centre. Effective pitching and presenting requires you to be able to highlight your relative competitive advantage.

Promoting the height and fitness of your security guards has little relevance when being compared with networked cameras. Instead highlight the advantages of seeing people on site and the extra roles that guards can perform – this is more likely to have an impact on decision-makers.

Market mapping is a useful technique in helping to get an overview of the market space you are operating in. It is also a good way to get a lot of the information that is in the team's head on to paper.

Don't try to draw market maps at the whole business level but rather focus them around the segments or sectors of the market you are concentrating on. Although you may find the same main competitors in each part of your market, there will usually be differences in who is the leader or most aggressive in a particular sector. Similarly, the drivers of change and market dynamics are also likely to vary.

A market map identifies the key competitors and can be annotated with metrics that help you get a picture of the overall market.

Opposite, we have a simple market map for specialist print services (fast turn-round company reports). In this illustration four companies compete for this market. The inset figures show the estimated market share of each of the players. There are three ways in which contracts are awarded – direct selling, repeat business and a process of tendering and pitching.

Some 20% of the £55m market is allocated by tender and pitches, which currently only companies A, B and D are competing for.

Such maps can potentially contain a lot of information. Use arrows to indicate the direction of change, and add market shares by channel and any market segmentation variables.

Market maps are descriptive rather than analytical tools and are useful in helping to encourage teams to consider the strategies of key players, alternative routes to market, etc.

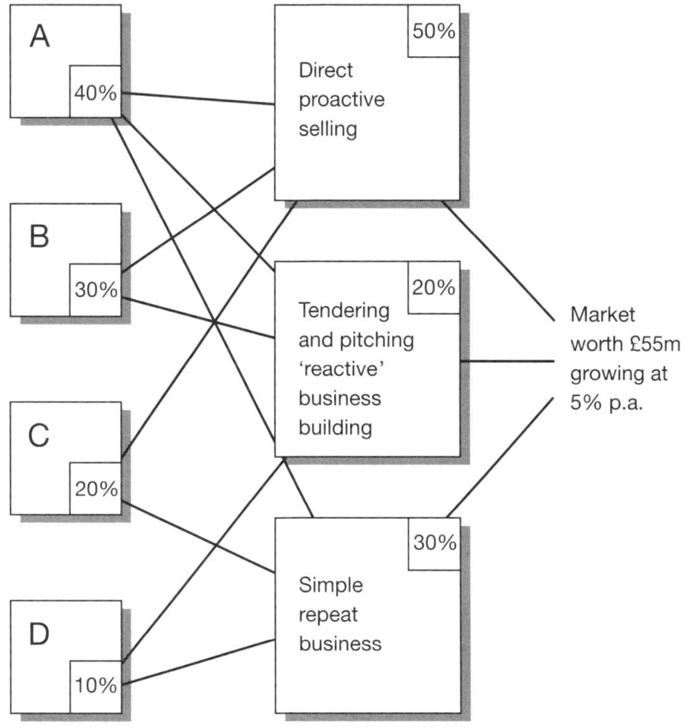

Choose a market you are active in and try to draw your own market map. Work with colleagues to add as much detail as possible.

Next think about what insights this gives you about opportunities to compete.

Set up competitor watchers

Competitive advantage is assessed by the customers in the context of your competitors' offer – literally, who satisfies their buying criteria at the best price. It is certain therefore that you cannot afford to ignore what your competitors are doing and how they present themselves. Your performance will be measured against theirs.

Once you have identified the key competitors, you can start to build up your understanding of them and their strengths and weaknesses. You know they will be highlighting their strengths and your weaknesses in their presentations and pitches. Like a good football manager, studying the competition should be a starting point for developing competitive strategy and tactics. There are a number of techniques for illustrating the differences between competitors – the spidergram is a popular method. With a spidergram you use its arms to represent the customer's buying criteria. You can then rate the performance of you and your competitors in terms of each of these.

Functional performance

0 1 2 3 4 5 6 7 8 9 10

You create a spidergram by identifying the key buying criteria in your market – price, availability, service, functionality, image, after-sales support, etc. You then rate on a scale, say 0–10, how well you deliver each of these benefits.

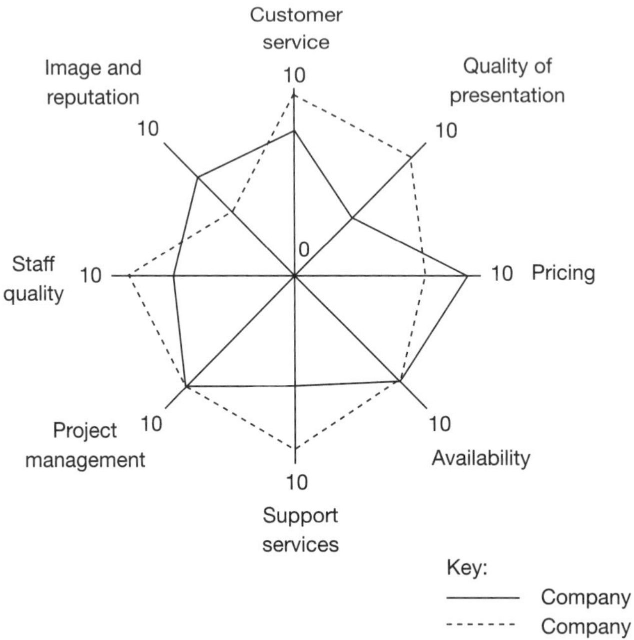

There is an arm for each of the criterion – you plot your position on each and then join all the positions together to create the web that illustrates the strength of your bid. Doing the same thing for each of your competitors and overlaying their webs (different colours help) allows a visual assessment of the relative strengths of you and your competitors.

Spidergrams allow you to add several competitors and their relative strengths or potential competitive advantage become clear. In this example company B may be a little more expensive but the quality of their presentation and better service and support backed by staff quality could well win them the business.

The weakness of this spidergram is that it implies that all the buying criteria are equally important. To create a more realistic picture you can alter the length of the spider's arms to reflect the different weighting of each criterion.

The following spider's web represents a customer's ideal offer.

It is not enough to collect lots of facts and figures about your competitor – knowing their head office location, number of staff or the eye colour of their security manager is unlikely to help much when it comes to winning business. You are looking for insights into its strategies, tactics and performance. You must be

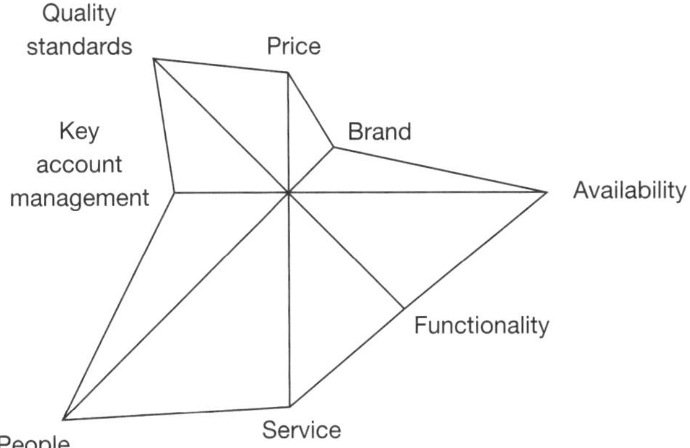

Set up competitor watchers by allocating a named competitor to each member of your team – even those with no direct sales/marketing responsibilities, like the finance and HR managers, benefit from this. Each watcher takes responsibility for monitoring and reporting on a competitor – its behaviour, strategies, success and problems. Ask watchers to make a point of monitoring which competitive pitches are won and why. When faced with a pitch against a competitor the key information needed for preparation will then come from a single source. Here is a checklist of competitor information sources:

- **annual reports and websites;**
- **press releases (often stored on websites) and media comment;**
- **stands at exhibitions and trade shows;**
- **customers and suppliers – just talk to them;**
- **competitors' staff who join your organisation;**
- **'mystery shopper' research where you act as a customer.**

A competitor watcher working for an IT consulting company spotted that a key competitor was advertising for a director of project management and a support team of qualified project managers. This information gave his company advance warning of the competitor's strategy to build competitive advantage on project management capabilities.

selective. When you get new information, or when planning to get new information, ask 'So what insight does this give me?'

Where does customer information come from?

Research with customers is the best way of finding out about the customers' buying criteria. Focus groups and in-depth discussions are likely to be the most useful methods, but remember that there may be several people with different agendas involved in the buying decision. Other insights can come from observations in the market.

- What happens to the volume of demand if you reduce your price, perhaps as part of a promotional offer?
- When the competitors hire a high-profile project manager, how much more often do they win contracts?
- How do customers respond to a firm's offer of improved functionality or better service levels?

Nothing beats talking to customers if you want to understand what matters to them. Dialogue, in its many possible forms, is key to customer-centric business and your sales teams are ideally positioned to bring such insights back to your business.

Below is a checklist of methods for getting to know your customers better. Which do you use currently, and which could you adopt to increase your understanding and insight?

Method	*Currently use*	*Could use*
Organise customer user-group workshops or forums		
Appoint staff to work in customer organisations observing your product/service in use		
Focus-group research		
Attend trade shows and events aimed at your customer's clients		
Join or support the activities of your customer's trade association		
Employ staff who have experience working in the same sector/area as your customers		
Organise briefings from consultants or other third-party experts who understand the customer's sector and the driving forces impacting on it		
Invite customers to help to develop the next product or presentation through formal and informal collaboration. For example, websites can be used to get feedback on new product concepts or to ask people to vote for preferences, etc.		

Waiting your turn to speak is not the same as listening. It is easy for organisations to believe that their expertise in an area is the same as knowing what is best for the customer. In such circumstances, dialogue offers an opportunity to tell the customer what they should want – but equally, failing to hear what the customer is telling you really matters. Use third parties to facilitate dialogue if this is a problem.

Knowing what the customer needs, wants and talks about today is only half of the picture. You also need to be prepared for what they will or might want tomorrow. This requires forecasting and asking questions about how things might be changing.

A firm that produces packaging solutions for the electronics sector makes a point of attending leading international electronics fairs every year. At these events new developments are showcased and this gives the firm advance warning and insight into the future packaging problems of their customers. As an added bonus they get to network with current and potential customers exhibiting at or visiting the fair and this gives them something in common to talk about when meeting later. In turn the customers are impressed that the company has shown interest in their industry – an important step in building a strong relationship.

This should take only ten minutes. Choose one of your clients or customer segments and list three ways in which its product or business might change over the next five years. For example a contract publishing services company might face:

- falling revenue from magazine-based job advertising as the process migrates online;
- reduced average production costs owing to advances in new technology;
- growing demand for e-publishing skills and services.

If you found this difficult then it means that you don't know enough about your customers and need to take steps to understand their business and to share this understanding with your colleagues.

Include sector and competitor briefing sessions in your regular team meetings. Don't try to do too many at once and also be innovative in your presentations to make them more memorable. If possible run 'meet the customer' sessions where invited customers come along to tell you about themselves, their challenges and future industry developments.

The advantages of small business

One of the reasons that smaller organisations are often successful is they know their customers. Senior management are in regular contact with customers, meeting them on the job and going out for a drink with them. As organisations grow they have to make an effort to retain this customer intimacy.

 Digging for detail

So far, the information we have been discussing is at the macro level. Its been about the industry and big changes impacting on all the players in that space. Some of this comes from general awareness of the business world through the media and some through specific research and observations. So, for example, if you were going to meet a senior manager in an NHS Trust hospital you would probably know that:

- she will be concerned about meeting government targets;
- increased patient choice and new methods of ensuring that funding follows patients means that marketing is increasingly important;
- budgets are tight and so cost-effectiveness will be implicit in all decisions made.

What you don't know is the detail of that Trust – who's who, how it is performing and what the local issues and challenges are.

Mobile operations
A company that provides mobile operating theatres for hospitals can help to solve a variety of problems. For example:

- it can provide extra staff capacity to tackle bottlenecks and waiting lists, thus ensuring targets are met;
- it provides alternative capacity when hospital theatres are being refurbished or are out of action for other reasons – in this case unstaffed units are preferred;
- it enables Trusts to provide services locally, even in the furthest reaches of their catchment areas.

Knowing in advance *why* the Trust has made an enquiry about mobile theatres will make a big difference to how the proposal is phrased and the benefits highlighted.

In this case, research using the Trust's website provided details of the redevelopment plans and how many theatres were likely to be affected over the next three years.

 The brief – the information starting point

The brief is perhaps the most important source of information you have when it comes to establishing the specifics of a customer's needs. This brief can come in a number of formats.

- The **invitation to tender** – a very formal document which will contain the specification of what is required. Sometimes opportunities exist for questions and clarifications but normal practice is for this supplementary information to be shared with all those tendering.
- The **written brief** – a less formal document, the quality of which depends on

the skill of its author. If the brief doesn't cover the basic contents you will need to seek clarification.

Structuring a brief

- **Background** – includes all relevant details and data, research and past experience.
- **Purpose** – what is being done and why.
- **Requirements** – the supplier's role in this process including any job specifications minimum standards, etc.
- **Process** – an indication of:
  - how selection of a supplier will be made;
  - how you will work with the selected company, for example the frequency of meetings, decision-making structures, etc.
- **Constraints** – any of these need to be clear in terms of:
  - timing
  - budget
  - other factors, for example a required methodology or ownership (for example, a piece of research that the client may want to be able to publish later).

- The **verbal brief** – this is the least formal and can be managed in a number of ways.
  - All those competing are invited to be present. There is a presentation of the brief and an opportunity for questions.
  - Each potential supplier is met individually and briefed. In this case early preparation concerning the client is key, as your questions and answers could help you obtain a more useful or detailed understanding of the needs than your competitors get. This information advantage will provide you with a chance to gain a competitive advantage.
  - The brief is given over the phone. It can be helpful to record this but remember to tell the client that you are doing so. This leaves you free to focus on what is being said and the questions you should be asking. Alternatively, use a speaker phone or conference call system and ask someone else to take notes.
  - The brief takes the form of a dialogue between you and the client. Your knowledge and questioning techniques will be key in ensuring that you get the information you need. Use the structure of the brief above to give you a framework for questioning.

In any case, when no written brief or specification is given it is good practice to create one for yourself and, if possible, ask the client to review it to ensure that you have understood their needs and all the issues.

Internal projects

The lack of a formal written brief is characteristic of internal business projects, but the same advice applies. Once you have discussed the needs, constraints, background, etc. with the project stakeholders, structure your material into a brief and get it signed off internally. It saves many problems later if there is an agreed and evidenced consensus at the start of the project.

Adding the client specifics

Let us assume you have just received an invitation to tender or submit a written brief. Before you can evaluate the opportunity you may need some background details on the client. Make use of the Internet. Basic information about the organisation, its size, ownership, line of business and aspects of its strategy are likely to be there for you to download. For listed companies, look at their annual reports.

Don't forget the basics. Check out the creditworthiness of clients you have no track record with, and any potential currency or foreign exchange problems if the client is based overseas. Systems for doing this should be well established and be a routine part of your evaluation process.

The London Stock Exchange provides a free annual report service on over 1300 UK listed companies. It will deliver copies within 48 hours, or you can download the reports from its website www.londonstockexchange.com

And of course, double check your database to make sure that you have no history with this company. Remember, it may not have been a past client but you may have been shortlisted by it before. Talk to others who know the company and build up your picture steadily. As you do you will see the information gaps and you can go back and ask the client directly about these.

Consumer markets and the Internet

If you sell directly to end-user customers you may feel envious of the data available online to your B2B colleagues. However there may be more help for you than you think. If you are selling landscaping services or double glazing check out www.checkmyfile.com. Put in the client's postcode and you will get a general overview of the neighbourhood from housing types to an assessment of the financial risk of doing business with him or her – maybe enough to help you customise your presentation before knocking on the front door.

Organising your research

This research preparation is a vital first step in the process of winning business. How big a task it is depends on:

- the breadth of customers you serve;

- the quality of your internal information systems and databases;
- the number of business opportunities you need to respond to;
- the size of the team and resources available to you.

If this part of your current approach is relatively undeveloped you should:

- **not try to get it perfect all at once but build up your understanding of one sector of the business at a time – do the research on clients and opportunities in those areas and then monitor the impact your new insight has on conversion rates.**
- **make sure that you build an information system so that research done for one pitch or tender isn't lost but can be reused and built on when a further opportunity comes up in the same business area.**

However complex or straightforward the task you are faced with, you need to develop processes and guidelines so that the research aspects become routine and the work needed can be shared across the team.

An office-cleaning services company, run by three partners, was growing rapidly but the time taken in responding to tenders and pitching for new business was an increasing concern. The partners found that they were often working late doing the research needed to evaluate opportunities and customise their responses.

They introduced an information template – a simple front sheet that was put with an invitation to tender when it landed in the office. The receptionist was given the necessary training and took responsibility for collating information from the various sources.

The result is that when the file is handed to a partner for review and action, it comes complete with much of the available data.

Information needed

- Financial check
- Sector overview
- Past clients in sector
- Previous success rate in sector
- Client details
- Premises audit and number of staff

Who is responsible for this step in your process? Would this sort of approach help you spread the workload? Would the added structure help to ensure a consistent approach? If so, think about the information you would want added to your invitations to tender. Note that these information needs should reflect the specific needs you have when responding to an opportunity – for example, office cleaners need to know about number and location of offices and their size, indicated by staff numbers.

Managing your information

Use the following checklist to think through the type of information you need and the best sequence to collect it.

- Company profile – who is it, who owns it, where is it based, what is the business area and how extensive is its size of activities?
- Financial profile – does it satisfy credit checks, what is its turnover, growth and profit levels?
- What are the drivers of change in its sector?
- What is your experience and track record in that sector?
- Who are the likely competitors in this sector? What do we know about their strengths and weaknesses?
- What is the client's position in the market and what are the characteristics of its strategies as it impacts on your offer and area of interest?
- Who is whom in the decision-making unit for the company and what do you know about its culture?

Now:

- think about the possible sources of that information;
- train relevant staff to use these sources and present their findings;
- monitor how the information is used and review it at intervals in order to build in ongoing improvements;
- assess how better information improves your success rate – this gives you the basis of a business case if in future you want to improve your information sources.

Meeting the decision-making unit

Your research into the market and segment should have given you an idea of who typically are involved in the decision-making unit (DMU) along with their likely job roles, etc. Once you know, for example, that the premises manager, finance director and HR manager are likely to make up the unit, you can find out who holds these roles in the client company.

Check if the company is happy for you to talk to individuals like this, as a quick phone call will enable personal contact and allow you to check out their individual concerns and needs. Do take care, however, not to make contact if the rules of the tender or pitch expressly prevent it.

The kind of questions you should be asking include:

- What is the need and do we have case studies we can draw upon?
- What do we know about the:
  - selection process
  - location
  - timings

- audience (names and roles)
- requirements
- constraints?

Success lies in preparation

The better your preparation the better the finished job? Of course it takes time and effort but systems and processes can help to make it more manageable – and you must make it a priority.

Still not convinced research will make a difference to results? Then set up your own experiment. Do a thorough job on ten opportunities but not such a thorough job on another ten. Is the volume or value of work won different? Judge for yourself.

putting on the customer's shoes

A source of competitive advantage

Having a folder full of customer data and information will not, in itself, give you a competitive advantage. Only if you use this information to help you tailor the content and approach of your communication will it have an impact on the buying behaviour of the customer.

In today's challenging and competitive environments you might expect that all organisations would make customer insight and understanding a priority. In reality, too few do and many turn up to client meetings with little idea or apparent interest in the client's agenda. This indifference provides the more customer-focused teams with one of their greatest possible sources of competitive advantage – customer empathy.

In this chapter you will get the opportunity to turn your preparation and research into the ingredients that will make your messages hit home. It answers the following questions.

- What is empathy?
- How can you turn features into benefits?
- How do you use information and research to assess the customer's needs and agendas?
- What is emotional intelligence and how can you use it?
- How can you establish the parameters for ensuring empathy?
- How can you read body language to advantage?

Understanding empathy

Empathy is the ability to see things from other people's perspective – to appreciate their feelings and relate to them. This is a very powerful cornerstone in any relationship and is as important in business as it is in social relationships.

Some people are more instinctively empathetic than others. In whatever scenario, they are able to sense how those involved must be feeling and to sympathise with them.

The research you have just been undertaking enables you to visualise the scenario your potential client is involved in. Your role now is to think about what that means for those involved and, of course, how your offer or proposal will help or support them.

What's your advice?

Take a few moments to consider two scenarios. Perhaps you have experienced something like them yourself – if so you will be able to empathise with those involved.

Scenario 1

A management trainee has been with the organisation for 18 months but is gradually becoming demotivated. Initially highly enthusiastic and eager to suggest change and new ideas, her line manager is more pragmatic and prefers to keep things on an even keel. Performance isn't great but it is steady and that makes for a quiet life – everyone can go home at 5.30.

There is a new project being started in the department and the trainee has worked hard planning the details of a new methodology that will make implementation easier for everyone. She has researched this thoroughly and can show evidence of the savings others have made.

- What advice would you give her on the most effective way to pitch her proposal for change to the manager?

Scenario 2

Company A is pitching its services for outsourced call centre management to the management team of a national utility company. Until now the utility company has managed this customer interface internally and has won awards for its frontline customer service. A new CEO with a cost-cutting agenda has been the driving force behind an outsourcing strategy that is impacting on several areas of the business.

- How do you think the management team will be feeling and how would you advise Company A to approach this 'pitch'. Your audience will include the customer services manager and marketing director.

You can compare your advice with the comments at the end of this chapter.

Turning features into benefits

Perhaps the single biggest clue as to whether a company is client focused or not can be found by listening to a sales pitch or reading promotional literature.

The product-oriented and internally focused organisation will promote the many and varied features of its offer. The externally focused competitor will peddle the more compelling list of customer benefits. Experts and technically qualified people who take on the sales role often find it very difficult to be benefits focused. After all, their basic training was in the technology – they know how and why the product works, what it's made of and why this is a good choice of raw materials. For those who are not wholly comfortable with the role of the persuasive communicator, the product details represent a safe territory – a space where they are expert.

Neither is this product orientation limited to those with high-tech products or tangible offerings. The management consultancy can be as bad, promoting how many of its consultants are MBAs, the various locations of its global offices and the impressive line-up of past clients.

Of course features matter. They provide the basis for competitive advantage but the customer is interested in the benefits they deliver – the outputs rather than the inputs. The empathetic communicator features relevant benefits throughout his or her persuasive communication.

Turning features into benefits

Turning features into benefits is easy – you simply need to remember the phrase 'which means that'; then take each feature, add the phrase and the answer is your benefit. For example:

- **all wood is from sustainable sources *which means that* your environmental policy is fulfilled;**
- **all our projects have a dedicated project manager *which means that* you have a single point of contact and the progress and integration of activity is assured;**
- **our technology delivers a 10% performance improvement *which means that* you can save at least 10% of running costs;**
- **this approach has been shown to increase staff retention levels by 15% *which means that* we can expect to save £*y* on recruitment and have the benefits of more experienced staff in the team.**

Try this for yourself – choose a product, service or business case, list its key features and use the *which means that* formula to turn them into benefits.

You might then order your list to see which benefits are most important to a named customer, or which are most relevant to different people within your decision-making unit.

The ability to see things from someone else's perspective is known as *emotional intelligence*. In the business contexts that we are discussing, your understanding will often need to be more implicit than explicit. The audience will assess how well you understand both it and its needs by what you do and how you say things, rather by the words you use. This is why competition by tender is often so difficult.

More and more commonly the difference between competitors is not what they offer but how they do business. Questions such as:

- do we like them?
- can we work with them?
- do they share our values?

are as key to the decision-makers as the technical specification of your offer.

Choose a client, review all the information you have available and then try to assess what this means to the key participants in the decision-making team, how they will be feeling and how that might influence your presentation.

To make sure that you build empathy into your preparation, get the team together before the development of the presentation and brainstorm the implications of your research. Ask:

- **What issues are likely to be top of the customer's agenda?**
- **How will the key players be feeling?**
- **What would you want to hear if you were the customer?**

Interpreting research with empathy

Your research file will be full of clues that need piecing together and interpreting. One clue on its own won't tell you much but together they can build a rich picture. Look at the following examples.

Clue	*Interpretation*
The manager you are presenting to is newly appointed	They will be anxious to make a good impression – they may be trying to introduce change, but who they choose to work with will reflect on their decision-making capabilities. Brand, reputation and references may be critical.
The company has a reputation for innovation and a dynamic culture that supports it	It will hate bureaucracy and conservatism. Evidence of an ability to be creative through the look and approach to your presentation will be important. Pace and quality need to characterise your approach.
The pitch is for a pilot project in London but it is for a global company	Ensure that your approach is not too UK-centric – make the global scalability of your proposals implicit. Tackle explicitly any relevant issues of translation, intellectual property or cultural appropriateness. Because it is a pilot, measurement of success will be important – suggest the use of metrics and show how you can help evaluation.

Clue	*Interpretation*
The pitch is for the building contract for a major public building needed for a specific event in four years' time – the audience will be representatives of the trustees responsible for the project	Reliability and the ability to deliver on time and budget will be high on the agenda – too many examples of late and over-budget projects exist in the public sector. Examples, references and methodology may all be of influence. The audience will be difficult to manage with a wide range of individual and political agendas. It will not want to be associated with a failure – personal reputations are at stake.

Establishing the parameters

Building empathy into your preparation takes a certain amount of effort. It is almost inevitably lacking if you deliver an off-the-shelf company presentation or pitch. Start by answering some specific questions that should help you to customise your approach.

1 **What market/sector is the client in?**
This will help you to establish relevant language and terminology. The client is more likely to sense that you understand it if you are speaking the same language. So, if pitching to a GP talk about 'patients' not 'customers'; to a charity, 'shareholders' have little meaning but 'stakeholders' do; and a hotel will be concerned with bednights and occupancy levels rather than utilisation levels. It doesn't take much to pick up on key terms/phrases but it can make a difference.
It is the sector or market which will also have given you insight into the key drivers of change for companies in that sector – the things keeping them awake at night. What were they – globalisation? regulation? merger activity? new technology? In what way can your offer and presentation reflect these real issues for them?

2 **What is the nature of the client's purchase/need?**
What is it buying and why? But equally vital is how important is the decision to the client?
Remember that products are solutions to problems so in business-to-business markets all solutions should lead directly to lower costs, increased revenue and improved profit, or achievement of organisational goals. Are you clear on what the organisation's goals are and how your offer can help to achieve them? If you understand and respond to these needs you will have the decision-makers nodding in agreement throughout your presentation.
The importance of the decision makes a difference as to how people approach the decision-making process. In an earlier activity in this chapter, the decision for the newly appointed manager was more important because it was a first decision and would establish a reputation for making good or bad decisions.

Be careful to assess where the client is in the decision-making process. She may have already decided on a new conservatory. It is easy to fall into the trap of promoting the benefits of a conservatory when you should be focused on the benefits of a conservatory built by *you*.

As a rule of thumb the more expensive, infrequent and risky the purchase then the more people will be involved in the decision-making process and the longer it will take. Your approach can show empathy with this.

Three suppliers of printing systems were invited to present to a rapidly growing company. The approach was fairly informal and the level of bustle and activity is clear whenever there is contact with the business. There was a need for a quick purchase decision because capacity was becoming a constraint on growth, but this is a high ticket price item that will be business critical.

The three suppliers presented separately to the production manager, a technical consultant and the works manager. In terms of product, delivery and price there was little difference between them. The contract went to supplier 3 on the basis of perceived service levels.

Two suppliers had assumed that the decision would be made there and then. Supplier 3 had prepared summary notes of the key aspects of the purchase that were likely to be of interest to the owners and the finance director, including analysis of several pricing options and the return on capital employed.

This forethought demonstrated empathy with the management team and its needs.

The supplier who has empathy with customers understands:

- the implications of making the wrong decision;
- the significance of the cost as a percentage of income;
- the complexity of stakeholder considerations;
- the variety of factors that need to be weighed up in making the decision.

Decision making can be stressful, even when its not your money being spent. IBM's tag line 'no one was ever fired for choosing IBM' went to the heart of the buyers' source of stress in a business purchase. Putting yourself in your customers' shoes means trying to help them address or resolve some of these problems.

3 Who is involved over what timeline?

We began to touch on these parameters above but they are worth revisiting. You need to know and understand the agendas of those in the decision-making team and the stages of the decision-making process for that organisation.

The latter is to try to ensure that you aren't focused on the benefits of working with you before the customer has decided to work with anyone, and to ensure that you aren't trying to close a sale while the customer is still gathering and assessing information.

The notion of empathy goes further than understanding the company – you must relate to the people who represent it and address their functional and specialist concerns as well as their emotional ones.

In the decision to change to a new supplier of bearings in a large manufacturing business there may be a number of agendas to address:

- the production director will be concerned about performance durability and the impact on production quality or volume;
- the maintenance manager will be interested in ease of use, the speed of changing bearings and any training implications for the team;
- the finance director will be concerned with cost savings or financial benefits from improved performance plus stock costs and reliability of supply if downtime results in halted production;
- the HR manager may be concerned there are no health and safety implications of a change in supplier.

Your lists of those involved could be extensive but you need to be prepared to address all of them, directly or indirectly.

There may be many people involved in the decision-making process but they are not all equally important. In complex scenarios you might find it helpful to segment the client's team in terms of decision-makers' importance or influence in the buying process and the nature of their interest – is it strategic or tactical/operational? In other words do they care about how the consequences of decisions will impact on performance or how easy it will be to use?

Even in domestic scenarios the salesperson can feel the need to address the agendas of more than one person. Selling a loft conversion may mean assuring one parent that the staircase is safe for younger children and there is an exit in the case of fire, while the other may be concerned with disruption and guarantees of quality of work.

The different roles of members of a decision-making unit are summarised below.

Interest	*Significant influence*	*Less significant*
Strategic interest	Focus on big picture and performance issues	Acknowledge their interest but don't focus on them
Operational interest	Provide evidence of operational performance (provide details to this group separately if necessary)	Ensure they know their needs won't be neglected – reassure them

Providing headline information in a presentation while providing details specific to key job roles in handouts can prevent people getting lost in technical detail. It also enables you to use the relevant jargon and terminology familiar to those specific job roles. This use of physical evidence proves that you recognise the importance and interest of these key people.

4 **The details of the brief provide the final dimension**
Make sure that you have understood, and demonstrate this to clients by recapping the key aspects of their specification or the constraints they have highlighted. This can often be achieved by being specific.

- 'We have a track record of delivering within three months' . . . sounds like an off-the-shelf statement.
- 'In the last six months we have delivered eight projects within three months – that is four weeks faster than the time frame you have specified' . . . sounds more like you can prove what you say and have listened to what they said.
- Much of this technique lies in personalisation of your message. For example, 'Delivery within 50 miles is within six hours of order received,' is anonymous compared to 'We can deliver to your Stockport depot within six hours of receiving your order.'

Review a past or future presentation or pitch and the documentation supporting it.

- How does it rate for evidence of emotional intelligence?
- Where and how could you add more empathy and personalisation?
- What impact do you think this will have on the audience?

Even the very formal tendering process allows you to use language to show that you have heard and understood the client's needs. Do not go over the top, but do look for instances where better phrasing could add impact.

About you or about me?

The problem with persuasive communication in a business scenario is that you are trying to sell yourself or your product. You want someone to know why yours is better than others and by how much!

I, on the other hand, don't really care about you. I care about me and my problems – you only come into the picture insofar as you can help me with my problems. This may seem selfish and one sided but this is a buyer's market and as a buyer I am more important than you – I can set the agenda.

Poor sellers often fail to recognise the reality of today's market. Many of them remember when things were different, when suppliers dominated the marketplace. Customers were grateful to be served and products were appreciated for their features and functions.

This misunderstanding of today's market, and the 'selfish buyer', results in many sellers presenting their case in the wrong way.

- **The opening** – let me introduce us and tell you about our hundred-year history and all the awards we have won.
- **The product** – this is what it is, the technological miracle that enables us to offer this great list of features.
- **The offer** – this is what it will cost you and when we can deliver.

Exaggerated perhaps, but in essence the whole pitch is about the supplier – the poor customer hardly gets a look in. It's a bit like going out to dinner with the proud new parents. You can sort of appreciate the miracle but it can get a bit one sided and boring!

The competitor who can put themselves in the customer's shoes understands this reaction and even empathises with the selfishness. What the competitor has to say may be essentially the same but the words are couched in terms that look at the world from the buyer's perspective.

- **The opening** – this is your world and your problem; we recognise its uniqueness and challenge and think we can help.
- **The offer** – these are the benefits we can contribute and how they will help you. This is what these benefits will cost.
- **Why you should choose us** – this is who we are and how we can help you. Here is our track record and the benefits it offers. This is our competitive advantage and how it addresses your agenda.

We will be looking in more detail at how to structure presentations but it is hoped that these two contrasting examples illustrate the difference that a focus on 'me' or 'you' can make.

Look and listen

Observation can provide a great many clues about clients. The opportunity to visit their premises to submit a brief or make a presentation needs to be treated as an 'information shopping trip'.

Clues about culture are particularly useful and it is easier to assess a corporate culture by visiting a site and meeting the staff, observing decor, processes, staff dress and office layouts. A modern, open-plan environment with a cafe-style reception area and casually dressed staff is clearly different from an organisation in which staff are in suits, the reception area is formal and managers have individual offices off an oak-panelled corridor.

Dress codes are taken seriously by organisations and mirroring the 'uniform' of your audience can help the perception that you fit in. Finding out about the dress code before giving a presentation is a good idea.

If you are selling to consumers in their homes you have the same opportunity to assess their interests and style and use this in your presentation to them. In any face-to-face meeting you will have the chance to observe the body language of your audience. Interpreting and responding to it will help to assert your empathy.

For example, the meeting with a manager who is constantly looking at his watch tells you he is worried about time. If he is concerned about being late for an appointment then he needs reassurance otherwise you will find he is distracted and not concentrating. If the presenter asks how much time is available or offers to cut short the details and to provide them separately, then this empathy is likely to be appreciated.

Become a people watcher – observe them from a distance, perhaps in a meeting or in a sales discussion. Look at their body language. Can you tell who is interested and who is bored? Who is agreeing with what is being said and where the objections might come from? In group meetings you may also be able to assess who holds the most influence or power.

Monitoring and interpreting body language becomes a habit. You can encourage your team to be more observant by asking questions about body language – who saw what and how was it interpreted. Add these to debriefing sessions – once people know that they will be asked for such details they will watch, and watching will soon become a habit.

Body language clues

There is plenty to learn about if you become a student of body language, but the following are some of the broad signals.

- Sitting forward is a sign of attentive listening.
- Sitting back, particularly moving a chair back from a meeting table, is normally a sign that the person doesn't support what is being said.
- Clock watching is a sign of boredom or concern about another commitment – you are taking too long.
- People who are fidgeting or have eyes darting around the room are nervous.
- Drooping shoulders is a sign of weariness or lethargy – they may have heard it all before or just don't care.
- Head down is often a sign of timidity – they don't want to attract anyone's attention, they are not likely to be strong influencers in the decision process. They may be junior or less-experienced members of the group.
- The space that people take up is an indicator of power and influence – standing and moving around occupies more space; those who spread their arms on the chair and spread their papers around give the same impression.
- Hand-to-face movements – for example, scratching the nose or cheek – is believed to be a positive sign in a sales context. It is interpreted as a buying signal with a 'but' attached. Faced with this behaviour you need to ask questions to determine the objection or concern.
- Watch out for changing postures – the person with folded arms, crossed legs and who is turning away from you is showing signs of disinterest and lack of trust. If, during your presentation, they unwind, opening their posture and turning towards you, this is a sign that they are warming towards your theme and

beginning to trust you. Needless to say, movements in the opposite direction are not positive in a selling scenario.

- It is known that people are attracted by people who seem to be similar to themselves. This can be used to advantage in a sales situation by mirroring – copying the gestures and posture of the person you are talking to, nodding when they do, putting arms on or off the table and so on. Take care if you try to mirror because if it is done badly it sends strong negative messages to the receiver.
- Hand gestures are used to add emphasis and so can be seen to represent a strength of feeling.
- Eye contact is important and it has an impact on confidence levels. Limited or shifting eye contact makes us feel uncomfortable. Shaking hands firmly and making eye contact with the individuals you are presenting to can help to build a relationship with each individual and is a good first step in winning their support.

Remember that interpreting body language is an art rather than a science. People who understand body language can manage their own behaviour in order to influence the perceptions of others.

The nervous presenter

A colleague made a point of congratulating a new team member on her first sales presentation. 'You did really well, the audience liked you and you came across as very confident. No one would have guessed you had only been with us for two months. I thought you said you were nervous – how did you do it?'

Her response was: 'Thanks for the feedback, but I was really nervous. I use body language to ensure that is not how others perceive me. These are the tips I follow:

- I'm in the room before the audience I'm presenting to – that means they are coming into my space, even if it's in their offices!
- I stand and move around a little during the presentation. Too much movement can be distracting but standing while others are sitting signals authority – in this context being knowledgeable.
- I make sure the room is arranged so there are no barriers, lecterns, tables or equipment between me and the audience. The lack of barriers indicates I trust them and have nothing to hide.
- I make myself have an open posture (keeping my hands out of my pockets – not fidgeting) and never cross my arms, which is another defensive signal. Trusting them is likely to encourage them to trust me.
- I meet each person as they come into the room and make direct eye contact with them.
- I make direct eye contact with anyone asking a question and lean forward as they speak to show that I am paying attention.
- I monitor their body language throughout to check that they are understanding and supporting.
- Oh, and by the way, I try very hard to fight the instinctive body language which would shout nervous and not sure!'

We will revisit the topic of body language when we look at presenting in practice in Chapter 10. For now remember that while absorbing the body language of others your own body language is saying plenty.

Body language is influenced by culture and it can be a significant cause of confusion and uncertainty when dealing with people from different cultures. If working with internationally based clients you should make the effort to find out what you can about their body language to ensure that you are not unintentionally offended and give no offence in return.

Summarising empathy options

Business success often depends on your ability to engage with and make an emotional connection with the prospective client. You want them to trust you, and even like you. For this to happen you need to understand them and their needs – and to demonstrate your empathy. You can do this by:

- understanding their business, knowing the hot topics and changes driving their business;
- using their language and terminology instead of your own;
- recognising the individuals involved in decision making and respecting and responding to their agendas and priorities;
- talking in terms of benefits to them;
- making them the central topic of conversation;
- using body language to help influence perceptions and interpret their behaviour and needs;
- fitting in with their culture and mirroring their behaviour to be seen as 'one of them'.

Take a few minutes to list three things you can do from now on that will improve your empathy with customers.

Answers: What's your advice?

Scenario 1

The line manager is conservative and for whatever reason values a quiet life and is likely to be risk averse. If the trainee recognised that, her approach would be not to highlight the newness of the methodology but the benefits of an even easier life – going home at 4.30!

Using evidence from her research to reduce any perceived risk associated with the change, the benefits that need to be highlighted include:

- tried and tested
- proven
- resource saving.

I would advise the style of the pitch to be low key – as though it was no big deal. Physical evidence in the form of, perhaps, workflow diagrams highlighting the similarities (therefore minimising the differences) with the current methodology and case write ups with savings highlighted, would help to make the proposal seem more real and less new.

Scenario 2

Company A looks like it may be facing unwilling customers. The customer service and marketing managers are likely to be concerned at this change – they may be angry and feel their past efforts and successes have been ignored. They will be concerned that outsourced services mean a lowering of standards, loss of control and ultimately an increase in dissatisfied customers, making their lives even more difficult.

Company A would be well advised not to approach this by promoting the benefits of outsourcing – it would look like that decision has already been made. Acknowledging management's previous achievements and high standards may be a good start. Senior managers need to know how they will still be able to influence/control this aspect of their operation – the emphasis should be on partnership approaches rather than a takeover bid. The methodology of how Company A plans to manage the service provider/client communications and relationship may be a more powerful message in the first instance than how many operators it can call on.

The benefits to highlight include:

- two-way communication
- service levels set by the client company
- a track record
- reliability.

Physical evidence might include service levels achieved for other clients and the headlines from the service level agreement.

preparing to pitch

From building blocks to business

Setting the scene

Setting the strategy

Preparing the team

Who does what role?

Know your team

Briefing the team

Structuring the pitch

Added value and the bottom line

Timing

Using support materials

Practise, practise, practise

From building blocks to business

Our work so far has been the groundwork, looking at the building blocks of effective persuasive communication. In the following chapters we will focus efforts on the processes and techniques that turn those building blocks into new business.

In this chapter we will look at preparing to pitch and in the next at making the pitch. This is a step-by-step guide which you can use or modify to meet the specific context of how pitches are used in your business.

This chapter answers the following questions.

- What should you expect during a pitch?
- How do you prepare a strategy for pitching?
- How do you prepare your team for a pitch?
- What materials do you need to develop?
- What is the best way to structure a pitch?
- How do you prepare your arguments and deal with objections?
- What are the final preparations?

Setting the scene

No two pitches will ever be the same. Who is involved, what is expected and the environment will always be different, possibly influenced by culture, the purpose of the pitch and the personalities of those involved.

If you have done your homework you will be starting your preparation with answers to these questions.

- **What is the purpose of the pitch in this opportunity?** Are we pitching having been shortlisted or to get shortlisted? Is the pitch to allow the client to choose between competing suppliers or to decide whether or not it is in the market at all? Is this pitch intended to showcase our past work or to outline our proposed solution to their problem?
- **What are the rules of the pitch?** How long do we have, what space and resources are available to us, who will be there? We might also know if others are pitching on the same day and whether we can set up equipment in advance.

Pitches and presentations in other people's environments will always be challenging. If you feel that you don't have enough information about the available technology or support, the arrangements or access for setting up then do go back and ask for clarification.

- **What is expected from you?** This will have been spelled out in the brief but it is important that you manage and meet or exceed expectations on the day. If clients are satisfied with how the pitch went – they got out of it what they wanted – then they will feel more confident that you will deliver the contract they have on offer.

- **Who are they?** You should have your file of information and research on the company, its market and, hopefully, the key individuals involved. As we saw in the previous chapter, this is important in influencing your approach and style.

If you haven't got answers to these four questions your preparation is not complete and you are not ready to start preparing for the pitch.

You might like to turn these four questions into a template to be appended to the front of the brief so that you can be sure that all questions are answered before you get to work on the preparation.

Setting the strategy

In any planning process, strategy is crucial because it sets direction and ensures that everyone is pulling in the same direction. It is not enough to have the same objectives:

- to get shortlisted;
- to win the contract;
- to get a pilot/trial agreed.

The strategy spells out how you are going to *achieve* this goal. If some of the team are trying to win on price and others on level of service then the messages sent will be confusing. A good piece of persuasive communication has a few simple messages delivered consistently.

Content
Simple messages built on demonstrated competitive advantage and relevant benefits. You give them a reason to say 'yes'.

Delivery
Coherent, well-structured and demonstrates empathy. The client's team relates to your people and the presenters are passionate and trusted.

A successful pitch. The reasons to say 'yes' are compelling.

There are two dimensions to a pitching strategy:

- what you are going to say;
- how you are going to say it.

To develop your strategy you therefore need to consider:

- Content
  - what the client's problem is and what benefits it will value;
  - how your offer helps the client;
  - why your offer is better and more relevant than that of your competitors.
- Delivery
  - what the culture is and what the constraints of the pitch are;
  - what approach is likely to be memorable;
  - what arguments and style will be most persuasive;
  - how you can build empathy into your delivery.

At the height of some of British Rail's worst problems in the 1980s it was looking for a new advertising agency. A favourite anecdote at the time was about the strategy adopted by the team who was successful in winning the business.

The scenario

The BR decision team arranged to hear the pitches of shortlisted agencies in the premises of each of the agencies. Although many of them were in close proximity in Soho, the schedule was tight and keeping to time was a challenge.

Content	Delivery
Choose us because we understand what it s like to be a BR customer.	On arrival at the agency the BR team is met by a bored receptionist, asked to wait and told nothing despite repeated requests.

It's not hard to imagine how this high-profile team felt – frustrated and even angry. Only when the BR team eventually got up to leave did the pitching team put in an appearance with the very simple but powerful message:

'We know how your customers feel'

– left waiting, with no information, and staff who seem uninterested.

A high risk strategy – but it would certainly have been a memorable delivery. And, like most companies, BR would value working with an agency which demonstrates empathy with its customers.

Try this before going any further with the preparation for any pitch or presentation. In one sentence for each, answer these two questions:

- Why should they say 'yes'?
- Why will they remember us?

When you have answered these two simple but challenging questions you will have a strategy.

Revisit a few recent pitches you have made. Was there a clear strategy? How could your content and delivery strategy have been different?

Preparing the team

Once you know what you need to convey and the impression you want to make, it is time to put your team together. You need to address these questions:

- how many in the team?
- who should be involved?
- what roles will each play?

Too big a team and you will swamp the client; too small a team may be interpreted as not taking the opportunity seriously. The team size chosen will always be a matter of judgement. The higher the value of the work and the more technically complex the offer then the bigger the team you are likely to have.

Look at those involved in the pitches on the client's side. If the finance director is on the list you will need to have someone who can deal with financial questions. If the health and safety manager is there, you need your own expert to respond.

In general, think about the audience and its interests and make sure that your team can cover all the areas likely to arise. One golden rule to follow is that if the audience is 'team buying' then you will do better if you do 'team selling'. The idea is that if your technician can talk to the client's technician, your finance expert handle any financial queries, then the buyer and seller can focus on the contract. There is obviously a cost implication in team approaches but if it improves your conversion rate it may be worth the extra investment.

Asked why he won so many of the business opportunities that he pitched for, the owner of a landscape gardening business put his success down to one thing. The competitors send their salesperson or turn up themselves to meet a client and scope the job. He never went alone. He always took with him the team leader who would project manage that job. He held the opinion that once a client has met the expert and likes them, he wins the work. The competition often fail to understand that customers are as concerned with **who** is working on their premises as with how good the finished garden will look.

When deciding on how many in the team, you could start with a list of the tasks needed – and don't forget the backroom jobs:

- preparing materials;
- doing the administration and organising logistics;
- managing equipment, technology and materials on the day;
- leading the pitch;
- handling negotiations;
- dealing with specific agendas;
- doing the follow up.

Of course all these tasks could be undertaken by one person but it can look more professional and help the occasion to run more smoothly if there is someone dealing with setting up PowerPoint or handing out materials while the presenter is focused on meeting and greeting, or handling questions.

- How many people do you normally involve in a pitch, and who decides who should do what role?
- To what extent do you think you currently have the right people doing the right things?

Who does what role?

This can be a challenging question to answer. The most senior people are not necessarily the best people to front the pitch.

Professional services companies, like accountancy firms and management consultancies, could learn a lot from the landscape gardener mentioned above. Clients in this sector often complain that they meet the senior partners at the pitch but then never see them again – the work is done by trainees and recently qualified MBAs.

Clients will generally feel more reassured if they meet the people they will be *working with*, so wherever possible they should be part of the team.

If, for some reason, those key people cannot be involved then think about how you can introduce them – a video clip, biography or anecdotal story that helps to bring them and their personalities to the fore.

Even the specialist salesperson may not be the best person to lead a pitch team. You need to think through the specific role that you want your sales staff to perform. It is not unreasonable for the salesperson to be the 'door opener'. Having found the opportunity they could now act as the facilitator, chairing the meeting of buyer and the operational team from the client organisation.

Even in scenarios where the salesperson is well equipped to handle the whole pitch, you might consider the impact and added value of a senior manager coming along to meet this potential client, lending support and political weight to any promises made about performance.

In highly technical areas it is likely that the salesperson will be joined by a technician who can manage product demonstrations and product reviews, but take care over what message this is sending.

A newly launched software product was competitively positioned as 'can be used by non-experts'. This was key in a sector where the necessary expertise was in short supply. Unfortunately, inadequate product training for the sales force globally meant that requests for demonstrations and review were held up until the product expert could be flown from Europe to do the demonstration.

Not surprisingly the clients became sceptical about just how easy it was for non-experts to master this product.

Know your team

Deciding on exactly who should tackle which pitches depends on knowing what is needed and understanding the resources available.

You need to audit your team to understand the capabilities and potential of each member. You can do this in a number of areas:

- product knowledge
- ability to handle issues on other areas
- industry/sector knowledge
- presentation skills
- negotiation skills
- technical skills
- social skills.

You need to be honest in your assessments. The shy technician may be a product expert but will never come across well in anything but one-to-one interactions. Your outgoing administrator therefore may be perfect for providing back-up support and orchestrating the process.

Not everyone will be great at everything but:

- **ensure you can cover all the key roles with a team effort;**
- **build your contingency plans by taking positive steps to help the team to multitask and to develop its skills in other areas. Even simple things help, like everyone knowing how to set up and operate the laptop and projector or the product demonstration.**

Remember that who takes what role tells the potential client something about your culture. If only the boss speaks, the perception will be of a hierarchical structure. If the pitching team are all white, male and over 50 don't be surprised if the audience makes assumptions about the rest of the staff.

To summarise on team size and composition:

- there should be sufficient people but not too many;
- choose the team to reflect the culture and needs of the audience;
- try to include those who will actually deliver the job for the client;
- use the team to add impact and memorability;
- try to include someone to manage the set up and provide support in the background;
- choose people for their current and potential presentation skills – but keep training them.

Of course, people sometimes do have to work alone. This does not reduce the work that needs to be done but it does make the need for rehearsal and a cool nerve greater. If you find yourself in this position:

- ask for ten minutes to get organised and plan before how best to use this time. If the audience will have to wait then provide materials they can review during the delay;
- make sure everything you need is ready to go, so far as you can – have extension leads ready and disk loaded. Practise using the equipment to get setup times to a minimum.

Briefing the team

One of the recurring challenges in business is communication – how do you ensure that everyone knows what is happening, what their role is and what progress you are making? Communication is the foundation of motivation, and when it comes to winning business the team must be confident, persuasive and motivated.

The form of any briefing will depend on the size of the team, the complexity and value of the business opportunity and the culture of your organisation. You might like to consider some of the following.

- **Team briefing** – bringing the team together at the start of your pitching project is a good idea if it is feasible. People's time is valuable, so such briefings need to be structured and well managed. It is important to be clear what your purpose is:
  - What is the opportunity, the company, culture profile?
  - Who has what role in the team?
  - What are the objectives and what is the strategy for winning?
  - What is the timeframe and what are the milestones?
  - What are the details of the brief and client needs?

  Additionally you need to be sure that the team can access research data it might need to complete its part of the preparation.

You might find it more effective to organise several briefings so that different staff members are briefed only about their part of the process. So, for example, an advertising agency working on a new contract might brief the creative team who will develop the storyboard and creative solution to the client's brief. The briefing of the team chosen for the presentation can be carried out later.

- **Conference calls** – an alternative, which can help if staff are distanced and getting together before the pitch is difficult, is to consider a telephone-based conference call. E-mail the basic details to participants beforehand and use the call for clarification and answering specific questions.
- **Written briefs** – these have a number of advantages:
  - information can be structured, and if a standard format is used staff will get used to it;
  - everyone in the team gets the same information;
  - people can refer to this information later, helping to make misunderstanding and poor memory less of an issue.

  The disadvantage is the lack of question and answer opportunities and the reduced opportunities for chance team input and ideas at this stage in the process. To get the best of both worlds provide the team with a written brief as well as a face-to-face meeting.

Get a small project team together to assess your current briefing processes. Structure a standard process and the documentation needed and then recommend modifications to help improve your approach and build more customer centricity into your activities.

Structuring the pitch

While keeping the agreed strategy in mind, it is now time to start preparing what you are going to say and in what order.

Golden rule
Keep it simple: audiences can only cope with a few messages.

There is not usually a shortage of things to say. The challenge is to choose a few key messages that you are going to focus on. This means that there are things you could say but will choose to leave out. This process of selection can be very challenging. You can kid yourself that more is better, but it isn't. It is *not* the number of sales points you make that determines how compelling a sales pitch is, rather how relevant to the client the points are.

To help you organise your potential material start with a broad structure, a series of headings which you can populate. The detailed structure will vary but try to organise your material in a sandwich. This can be powerful:

- **persuasion** – why you need us (and not someone else);
- **content** – what we will do for you (the benefits);
- **persuasion** – why you should say 'yes' to us (the competitive advantage).

The fact that you have been invited to pitch indicates that the client knows you are broadly competent and meet its core and expected criteria. Spending some time telling the client you are a legitimate contender is probably a waste of opportunity.

Notice that the content of all three sections of the sandwich – persuasion, content, persuasion – is oriented towards the client. Under these three headings you can start to organise what has to be said. Your content might include:

- **Why you need us**

  Start by thanking the audience for the opportunity to pitch. Tell it what to expect – the duration and structure of the pitch – and what you are going to tell it. Introduce the team members and their responsibilities. Outline how questions will be handled.

  Set the context of the need/problem in sector, market and company terms. Remember that your audience will know this so not too much detail is needed – it simply needs reassurance you understand the issues. There may be an opportunity to point out that other organisations or customers faced with similar problems have been helped by you.

Your intention should be implicit rather than explicit in providing the audience with details of your credentials. You could give it a lengthy past-client list but this will be as interesting as film credits.

The design team for a major manufacturer of customised conservatories went to a client's site to take the brief, measure up and take 'before' photos. When it returned to present and pitch its proposals for the design it started by reconfirming the key elements of the client's requirements and then showing the client audience a selection of 'before' and 'after' shots of past projects with similar needs and requirements. This approach served several purposes:

- it showcased the company's quality of design and finished work;
- smiling clients in the pictures acted as silent referees;
- it highlighted the customisation process and the benefits;
- it provided evidence that the company did indeed finish the job – this reassurance is important with domestic building services.

The team found that just ten minutes spent looking at and discussing these other projects settled the audience. It was then ready to consider its own proposals in a more positive and relaxed way.

◆ **The content**

This is the meat of your persuasion sandwich, but remember to keep the client as the focus of your content. The detailed content will depend on how the pitch is used and what needs to be presented.

Having outlined the problem, describe what you can do to help resolve it:

- describe your methodology and approach to the problem;
- outline your proposed solution;
- discuss issues of implementation;
- open the platform for questions.

> **Keep technical details to a minimum and provide them in hard copy form so that they can be reviewed in detail at the client's leisure.**
>
> **Physical evidence such as this is important. It provides a tangible reminder of you and your pitch and adds tangibility to intangible services. A schematic of workflow or project planning processes can usefully demonstrate your grasp of *all* the elements of the project.**

If you are presenting a solution or methodology this is where your competitive advantage must be evident. Help the client see how your solution resolves its problem and satisfies its needs. Use the 'which means that' technique. For example, the ergonomic design of this machine *means that* it is easier and more comfortable to operate; you can be assured there is less likelihood of repetitive strain injuries.

Point out how your approach is different and better than that of the competitors. Remember to keep this message simple. Focus on just a few selling points. These might be aesthetic design, quality finish, reliability or service levels.

Demonstrate each of these and show the superiority of your offer in each area. Point out how this benefits the client.

Finally, summarise your key selling points to help the client to remember them.

◆ **Why choose you?**

They have seen your work and sampled your ideas but this final section is your chance to tell them why they should say 'yes' to you. Key points are:

- detailing your team and stressing its credentials;
- highlighting your organisation and its brand, quality standards and client list;
- describing your method of working in terms of communication with the client, milestones, problem handling and service guarantees;
- being clear about costs and options.

In each case make sure you point out why these factors matter to the client – for example, quality standards provide reassurance, and your methodology ensures that the client can influence the work in progress.

The key to customer satisfaction lies in the perceived balance of power – customers like to feel in control. You can give them control through choice. This works in negotiations through to handling complaints. Instead of saying, 'Here is our proposal and this will be the bill' try saying, 'You can choose between the basic solution at a price of £X or the added options for a price of £Y.'

This is an important point for marketing teams to recognise. Too often the only negotiating point given to sales teams is discounting. Alternative value added or value reduction packages would give both greater flexibility and enhance the customer's satisfaction with the service.

Added value and the bottom line

When putting an offer together and building in choices and opportunities for negotiation, price discounting should be a last resort position. Adding value is almost always more profitable than cutting prices. The trick is that the 'value added' has to be valued by the customer or it won't influence its buying behaviour.

Imagine that you have a product that normally sells for £1000. Its direct costs are £500 and every time you make and sell one there is a contribution of £500. This is the contribution to fixed costs and profit.

If you reduce the price by 10% to £900, the contribution falls by 20% to £400. Depending on your profit margins, such a situation may not be sustainable for long.

The alternative is to add value. Imagine instead that you promote a special offer that gives £1100 worth of product for the bargain price of £1000. Direct costs have increased by 10% but the contribution is higher, at £450. Customers perceive this as equal in 'value' to a price discount.

This is the financial basis of the BOGOFF (buy one get one free) offers in supermarkets, etc. As an added bonus, this approach does not change the client's perception of the price/quality position of the brand.

Look at what you could add to your offer that the customer might value – training to go with the new IT system, blinds for that conservatory or a free thirteenth month on the service contract.

But remember, the extra value must be valued by the client or it won't work.

Timing

Once you have a rough draft sequence for your pitch you can think about timings. Allocate approximate times for each key section and leave a few minutes contingency for overruns, etc. As a rule of thumb it is a good idea to use a 2:1 ratio of pitch to questions. So, if you know you have 30 minutes, the allocations could be:

- the problem – 2 minutes;
- the content – 12 minutes;

- why us – 2 minutes;
- questions and answers – 10 minutes;
- contingency – 4 minutes.

Using support materials

A sales pitch needs a sense of passion and belief and this is hard to generate if the speakers use cue cards and clearly haven't learned their lines! It is just not spontaneous enough.

This is where support materials are useful. They remind you of the script's sequence and ensure that you retain the logical structure of the presentation. PowerPoint and similar presentation packages can be either a boon or a disaster. There is little worse than 'death by PowerPoint'. Use the checklist on page 94 to ensure you use your presentation to support your pitch, not dominate it.

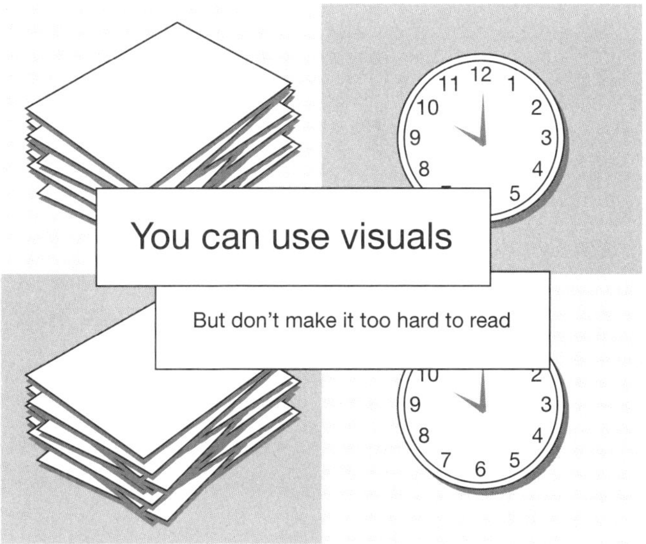

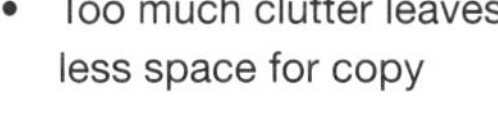

• Too much clutter leaves less space for copy

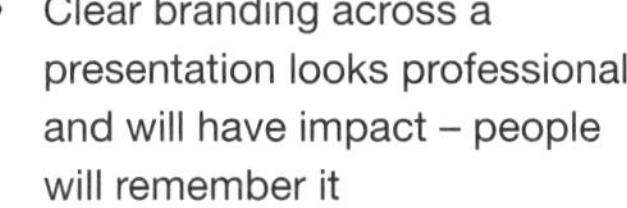

• Clear branding across a presentation looks professional and will have impact – people will remember it

• Make sure any images are relevant to the client

- Check that the facilities for presenting by PowerPoint will be available. You need space for the equipment, time to set it up, a laptop or access to a computer system and a projector and screen. Ensure that there is a power supply and extension leads if needed.
- If you don't already have one, develop a slide template that is consistent with your brand in terms of colours, typefaces, etc. You can customise your presentation by adding the client's logo to your master slide. Take care with the colours you choose. Remember that a surprising number of people are colour blind and that reading white on some colours can be difficult in certain lights. Try out your slide template for viewability.
- Keep copy simple – use summaries or key headings that the presenter can build on. If the presenter simply reads from the slide there is little obvious value added by the presenter being there. Provide additional detail, facts and figures in handout form.
- Keep type size reasonably large – 22 point at least – and use bold and italic to highlight titles or key information, but don't overdo it. Customise your slides so that one bullet point at a time is revealed. This keeps the audience focused on what you are saying. Avoid too many flying bullets or sound effects. Choose a reveal method – for example, appear from the right – and use it consistently.
- To help the presenter spot when all the points have been made, put a full stop only at the end of the last bullet point on a slide.
- Try to limit the number of slides to one every two minutes or longer – so ten slides for 20 minutes of pitching.
- Ask yourself what value each slide is adding to the presentation – make slides work for you. (See the examples opposite.)
- Use the 'notes' facility under each slide to help the presenters to add value, planning commentary to support rather than repeat the slide copy.

There was life before PowerPoint and in limited time slots or space, setting up the hardware can be surprisingly difficult. Suitable alternatives include:

- preparing a set of flipchart pages – be sure that there is a stand or some other way of displaying these;
- giving everyone a hard copy document with copies of slides and supporting materials – they can then follow this script and they have this as a tangible reminder of your pitch.

Other resources

You want the audience to interact with you and your organisation and to relate to you. Samples, materials and exhibits they can look at are really helpful – think about an architect's models, plans or paper samples. 'Before' and 'after' photos of previous work, a copy of your customer charter or storyboards relating to a proposed campaign are further examples. Every sector will have its own opportunities for involving the audience with complementary materials.

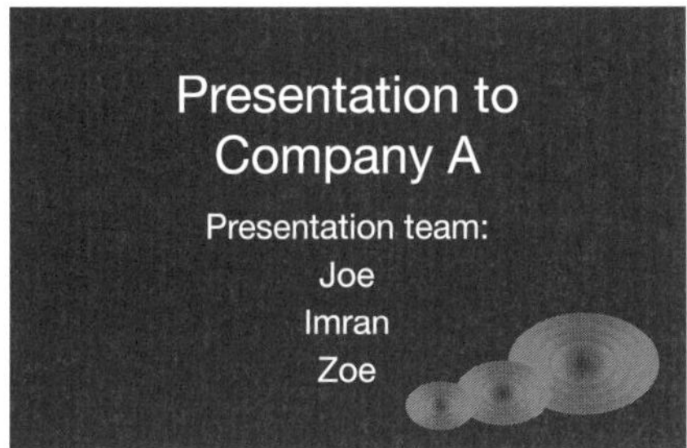

Building marketing skills with Company A

Your presentation team:

- Joe – your marketing strategist
- Imran – your account manager
- Zoe – your support co-ordinator

Making slides work for you:

- Slide 2 works harder than slide 1
- Client benefits are embedded into the title
- The title itself is a positive statement – implicitly confident
- Notice the use of 'with' in the title – establishing a partnership
- The use of 'your' helps to make a connection with the audience
- Roles as well as names help to establish the team's credibility

Plan your 'leave behinds'

While thinking about resources to support the pitch itself, consider also what you want to leave behind. You may decide to present a formal proposal document, leave samples, a copy of your presentation, a price list and/or referee details and the samples developed for them.

How you package and present these in a way which reflects the values and positioning you want to achieve deserves some thought too. Certainly these assorted materials need to have a coherent and integrated presentation to avoid looking like a lucky dip!

Practise, practise, practise

As the day for the pitch draws closer, the team needs to practise. Individuals can rehearse their own parts, and if more than one person is involved in the pitch then there must be at least one team run-through.

This is the last chance to get the details right so you need a stage manager or observer to provide you with feedback on the performance. If possible, video the rehearsal and review how everything comes across. Try to recruit a mock audience – giving members roles to represent the client's team members.

Rehearsal tips

- Start from the beginning – go to the room with your equipment, materials and bags to do the set up. Who is making introductions, handing out materials and so on?
- Check the time – set an alarm so you know when your 20 minutes is up. Ask one of the audience to time each section.
- Give the audience a checklist of points it should be looking for:
  - the strength of the selling messages;
  - the logic of the structure;
  - reasons to say 'yes';
  - areas for improvement;
  - the body language of the team.

  It is important that this audience is constructively critical – it needs to be briefed carefully and then given time for feedback to be listened to and acted on.
- To ensure the practice process is taken seriously, book it into people's diaries.
- Get the audience to ask questions. Spend time reviewing and tightening up on answers.
- Pay attention to how the individuals in the team work together. Is their body language supportive – are they listening attentively to each other's contribution? Make sure there is one person orchestrating the whole process, introducing and managing the pace. Handovers need to be planned and held in a logical place so the handover process is seamless.
- Try asking each team member to do the 'elevator pitch'. What are the key messages if your 20 minutes was cut down to just two?

If pitching is a routine and frequent part of your business activity, a full-blown rehearsal is not practical before each presentation. However, just as with driving, familiarity with the process can lead to complacency and bad habits creeping in. Try setting aside a time once every couple of months to do a full-blown practice, ideally videoed – we find it hard to accept our own bad habits sometimes. Use this to help to improve your technique and to maintain quality.

Throughout the practice process keep checking that your strategy is delivered so that:

- you give them a reason to say 'yes';
- you deliver in a way that makes you memorable.

pitching with punch

Just another pitch!

First impressions count

Managing expectations and time

Working alone – the salesperson's pitch

Choreographing the pitch

Involve the audience

Presenting complex data

Adding the price tag

Watching body language

Tackling questions

Don't be surprised

It's a question of money

Remember – a strong finish

About that impact

Next steps

Just another pitch!

The day is warm. An audience of five shuffle in their seats as a team of three enter the room and prepare to present. This is the third presentation of the day and there is still one more to come. They all cover similar ground, promising great service and highlighting their product's superior performance.

This is the sort of scenario that characterises pitches in many contexts. Even when the presentations are spread over a number of days the content will remain similar and there is the added problem of remembering who said what. If the client comes to your premises, the character and culture of your operation are evident and become a landmark to distinguish your presentation but – if you go to them . . .?

Well now your hard work and homework can pay off. Well prepared and rehearsed you will be in a position to concentrate on the performance and ensure it has punch. Punch that will give it impact and distinctiveness – both are key in the process of converting potential into business.

This chapter considers the following issues:

- the importance of first impressions;
- the questions of dress codes and gift-giving and the challenges faced by the international business team;
- how best to manage expectations and time;
- planning the choreography of the pitch, including how best to present complex data or detailed costs;
- the interpretation of body language and how to respond to it;
- handling tough questions;
- identifying ways of adding punch to your pitch;
- identifying ways of ensuring that you finish on a high.

First impressions count

This aspect of our behaviour is fairly universal – we meet someone for the first time and we 'size them up', we make judgements based on first impressions.

- Do they seem friendly?
- Are they well dressed?
- Is their handshake strong?
- Are they relaxed/confident/at home?

Our instincts have been honed over generations to help us to identify danger when meeting strangers – sometimes our first impressions prove to be wrong but, once made, they take time to alter.

In a business setting you may be meeting a number of new people at the same time in the formal and artificial setting of the pitch. It is really important to think about the first impressions you and your team are making. Equally importantly, you should think about the impression you want to make and how best to achieve that.

How do you want them to feel?

Imagine you are pitching for new business to a new client. You have an hour in which to present. Think about what impressions you might want to make over that 60 minutes – how do you want the client to feel about you? Try to allocate feelings to the different phases indicated.

Phase	*Time into presentation*	*Feelings about you established*
First impressions	0–10	
The presentation	11–40	
Questions and answers	41–55	
Closing	56–60	

You will find some feedback at the end of this chapter.

Those rehearsals, where you practised entering a room with bags, equipment and materials setting up quickly and efficiently, will pay dividends now. Your team will be working to a plan – a sequence of activities devised to ensure that the audience is engaged while you get organised.

We have previously recognised that you may have very little control over the logistics of a pitch and the selected environment. But if you do:

- **consider inviting the client to your facilities – but, of course, then take care of all the housekeeping details;**
- **ask if you can have early access to the client's premises in order to set up before the audience arrives;**
- **even if a separate room is not available you may be able to present first thing or immediately after lunch so you can get that time and space to prepare.**

Timekeeping

Punctuality is important, particularly when you are involved in a formal process like pitching. It makes sense to allow plenty of time and to arrive with a minimal amount of stress and strain. However, the question of timekeeping is not as straightforward if you are working overseas. In Russia, for example, *your* punctuality as the seller and visitor is expected but your host may keep you waiting, even an hour or more. This is seen as a test of your patience – so be prepared for it and do not react adversely to it.

In other parts of the world the rules can be different so do your homework – be informed so that you can manage your own and your team's expectations.

Meeting and greeting

If at all possible try to organise things so that the clients enter a space you already occupy – psychologically this will add to the perception of authority.

Make sure that you introduce *all* the team, even those in a support role. It is normal to introduce the most senior people first. It helps to include not simply job titles but an explanation of their role or contribution to the pitch. The client will be doing the same, telling you who is there and about their roles. It is easy *not* to pay attention at this stage – you may be thinking about what else needs to be said or done. The well-rehearsed team is more able to focus on the here and now, what is being said and by whom.

This is the first chance you will have to confirm that your research into who would be involved in the decision-making process is fruitful.

- Who did you expect to be present?
- Who isn't there and what was their agenda?
- Who is involved that you didn't expect? You may need to do some quick thinking to assess their likely agenda and interest, and modify your presentation appropriately.

Don't be afraid to ask questions at these introductions. Clarifying an individual's sphere of interest to probe his or her agenda will be seen as taking an interest, and the fact that you have recognised differences in the agenda of your audience is a positive.

Exchanging business cards at this stage is helpful and can be a useful prompt if you can't remember names easily. Have your cards ready.

International etiquette

Meeting and greeting and the exchange of business cards is strongly influenced by culture. No one should venture overseas without doing some basic research into what the custom and practice is in different parts of the world and, if in doubt, ask your contact in the company. Better to admit ignorance than give offence!

In China, for example, business cards are important. They should be offered and taken with two hands – proffered so the receiver can read the card. It is polite to study the card for a moment and not simply stick it in your pocket.

Researching business etiquette overseas is easy on the Internet – ignorance is no excuse for bad manners.

Making eye contact

A firm handshake, a warm smile and eye contact go a long way in creating good first impressions. For more junior staff, or the nervous or less experienced presenter, this may take practice. The meeting and greeting sequence may not last many minutes but it establishes early rapport. Remember, unless this is repeat business, both sides are trying to assess whether or not they *want* to work with each other.

Take care when pitching for repeat business – it is easy to take the process too casually. This, plus the familiarity with some of the decision-makers, can be perceived as being arrogant, or having an assumption the work will be yours. If they are going through a competitive process then take it seriously.

On home ground

If you are pitching to clients on your premises, pay particular attention to the details. A useful exercise is to brainstorm what can go wrong and what would make a difference to their welcome. Use the checklist below and add suggestions of your own for making those positive first impressions.

What can go wrong?	*What can you do?*
The client gets lost, is late, turns up at the wrong building	◆ Ensure that arrangements are clear and communicated in writing. Allow time for arrival and settling in – 10.00 for a 10.30 presentation. ◆ If dealing with international clients make it clear if it is UK time. ◆ Send location maps that are clear and include easy-to-follow directions – give estimated travel times. ◆ Include specific instructions about access, parking, the buildings and how to get in. ◆ Highlight a contact person and telephone number in case of problems.
Your visitors turn up at the car park to be turned away by security	◆ Double check if visitors are coming by car and how many parking spaces they need. ◆ Ensure that they know where the visitor's car park is and what to do if there is a problem. ◆ If there is no car parking then tell them what alternatives there are.
They get safely to reception but it seems that no one is expecting them	◆ Make sure that reception knows who these VIPs are. Give them a full list of names, as they may not travel together. ◆ Have security passes made up in advance. ◆ If possible use the notice facilities in the foyer to announce 'Our company welcomes your company'. ◆ Have someone designated to meet and greet at reception. This is particularly important if your team members are elsewhere setting up for the pitch. Do not keep visitors waiting. ◆ Try to ensure that the visitors feel that their business is valued – a welcome from a senior manager may be particularly appreciated.

What can go wrong?	*What can you do?*
They have had a stressful journey/morning/week	◆ You want the audience relaxed, feeling comfortable and focused. Give them time to settle in. ◆ Ensure that visitors know where the facilities are. Offer refreshments and a choice of when to make a start.

There is a code?

Remember that your first impressions were influenced by how someone was turned out. How would you feel if you went to see your financial adviser and he was dressed in torn jeans and a rugby shirt, or if your landscape gardener turned up in a three-piece suit?

Dress code does matter – it influences first impressions strongly. In some parts of the world appearance is even more critical. For example:

- in Italy clothes are a mark of success – good quality suits for men and elegant but quiet outfits are important for women; pay attention to the accessories, clean shoes, good quality handbags and briefcases; if you are seen as successful then what you have to say is more likely to be taken seriously;
- in Russia business people are expected to keep their jackets on during a meeting and never to loosen their ties;
- in China neutral colours and long sleeves for women are less likely to cause offence.

Again the advice is simple – if unsure of the etiquette then ask.

Team players or not?

Teams are often characterised by their uniforms – indeed, wearing a uniform can create the impression of a team. It also looks professional and gives a sense of coordination.

Of course not many organisations have a formal uniform that would be appropriate for the pitching team but a similar effect can be created with relatively little effort. For example, everyone wearing a similar colour combination of clothes, the men all wearing shirts and ties but not jackets, and so on.

When deciding on a dress code for presentations you should consider:

- **the culture and expectations of the client organisation – its corporate as well as national culture;**
- **the values and culture of your own organisation and how you want to be perceived.**

If these two are in conflict you need to consider the client's feelings first.

Earlier I asked how you would feel if your landscape gardener turned up in a suit. You might wonder if he could do the job – would he ever get his hands dirty? If it was a very expensive suit you might even look twice at the quote, perhaps thinking his dress was an indicator that his profit margin was on the high side.

Similarly, you wouldn't be impressed if he turned up in working clothes at the end of a day double-digging someone's new vegetable plot. Casual, but clean and tidy would be more in keeping with expectations.

Review how you and your team are turned out when they meet the customers and see if there is any room for improvement.

Gift giving

This is another thorny question that needs to be addressed and clarified for any client-facing team. It is another area where the rules change depending on where you are in the world.

The first thing to clarify is just what constitutes a gift?

- You might take the client to lunch, or to a corporate day out at an exclusive sporting event.
- A promotional gift with your company logo – a pen or calculator of limited financial value.
- A gift with a logo but also with a much higher intrinsic value – a new IPOD for example.
- A gift without a logo.
- The offer of a small payment in acknowledgement of the effort put in to helping set the meeting up.

The rules vary but you might use the quiz below to see what kind of first impression your gift-giving would make in the following scenarios.

What an impression

1 On arrival at the client's offices in Tokyo, you put on the table your carefully selected gift of four matching English crystal display vases, and after introductions push these towards the nearest member of the client team.

2 After a successful presentation, you offer your Chinese hosts a banquet to celebrate the conclusion of your first meeting.

3 You decide not to give gifts as part of your strategy when pitching to this Saudi Arabian client.

4 You know your main contact in this UK public sector organisation is mad keen on tennis so you offer her tickets to Wimbledon.

5 Whilst visiting a potential client in Italy, your contact invites you to his home for dinner with the family. You decide to take with you a dozen roses for your hostess.

You can check how your impressions compare by looking at the answers suggested at the end of the chapter.

In different parts of the world, and indeed in different organisations, the rules and indeed laws differ along with expectations. What is important is that you have clear policies on gift giving.

- What is acceptable and not acceptable should be laid down in policy and staff codes. That includes advice to staff working overseas.
- What is acceptable and expected in the client's country and organisation should be researched.
- Gifts need to be appropriate in terms of type and value
- Gift-giving should be transparent.

Gift accepting

Gift-giving is not a one-way process in many parts of the world so remember to prepare yourself and your team for being given gifts. Again it helps to have researched the protocol. For example, your Chinese client might ask you what you want. An appropriate answer is to ask for something that reflects the Chinese culture – an ink drawing perhaps.

Use the checklist below to help to ensure that your gift strategy does not hinder your business success. Make sure you know:

- who the receiving person or group is;
- what their status is;
- what is acceptable and what is not;
- what the protocol for the giving and receiving of gifts is;
- whether gifts should be reciprocated or not.

Managing expectations and time

To ensure that your pitch goes smoothly, it is important to manage both expectations and time. You may have had a brief allocating you a specific time, but it is worth:

- confirming this is still the case – 'I understand we have until . . .';
- sharing this with everyone – not all members of the audience will have been involved in the details.

People feel more comfortable if they know what to expect, so tell them – clearly.

- 'We are going to take about . . . minutes. During that time we will cover x, y and z.' Essentially you are telling them what you are going to tell them.
- Take the opportunity to introduce others – 'A will do x, B will speak on y.'
- Tell them what you won't cover – be clear about this and say why. For example, 'We are not going over the detailed specifications here because of time constraints but they are provided in your information pack.'
- 'We will have . . . minutes for questions and expect to finish about . . . o'clock.'

Now your audience knows what to expect. Members won't be worried about issues of costing or service because they know that is coming up later. They know how long things will last and so don't need to worry about missing a meeting or being away from their desk indefinitely.

Taking questions

Handling questions can be something of a dilemma. You need to make it clear from the outset how you want to deal with them.

- They can be taken as they arise. This gives a strong impression of expertise and confidence but it can make time management difficult. It can also result in a pitch without much sense of structure as the questions are likely to jump around from here to there.
- You can ask for questions to be kept until the end. This has the advantage of ensuring control and structure but it can be frustrating for the audience, who perhaps have simple questions early in the proceedings.
- You might opt for a compromise by providing opportunities for questions at the end of different sections of your pitch. Again, remember to flag this intention to the audience at the outset.

If you are experienced and confident, try asking the clients what they prefer – questions as you go along or all together at the end. Giving customers a choice makes them feel in control and is a good basis for building a strong relationship.

Working alone – the salesperson's pitch

So far the process of pitching has been discussed in the context of a team approach. In reality there will be many contexts and occasions when it is a single salesperson presenting and pitching to the client, be that a corporate or domestic customer.

The same rules apply – but with no back up your preparation is even more important.

- You need to be in command of your sales support materials – be they samples, a sales presentation or a demonstration in some form.
- You need to have easy access to all the relevant product and customer information. You need to know about the organisation and its relevant policies. For example, many organisations are concerned with corporate social responsibility and want to know about quality awards like ISO 9001 or Investors in People.
- You need to know about your organisation's current and future business strategy – what new products are planned and how that will impact on support and maintenance for this product?

First impressions really do count so, especially if working alone, try to keep your support materials to a minimum or integrate them into a single format. You need to concentrate on the customer rather than the technology during your limited time together.

Choreographing the pitch

This should also be planned and rehearsed and is as relevant to the single presenter as the team. Think carefully about:

- the benefits of one person being the front-man – introducing others, fielding and allocating questions, maintaining the pace and continuity. This works particularly well if there are many people involved in the process;
- how many 'voices' are appropriate. A cast of thousands can get confusing – leaving the audience wondering who's who and what their role is.

You may need a technical expert with you to handle very technical concerns and questions, but they don't necessarily have to present the case. You can introduce them without having everyone on stage.

- **If your presentation is supported by PowerPoint, use title slides to introduce each speaker, reminding the audience of names and roles. PowerPoint can constrain the flow of questions and dialogue but it does act as a prompt, reminding presenters of key messages and ensuring that the agreed structure is stuck to.**
- **If working alone use the same techniques to mark your transition from one part of your presentation to another – it helps the audience to follow the logic and structure of your messages. You can do this with caption slides, by announcing new themes or by taking questions at the end of each section.**

Remember that a range of speakers adds variety. If you are working alone you need to introduce variety in other ways – attention spans can be short, so make sure that you present with impact in a way that keeps people awake.

Involve the audience

Relationships need two parties. Involving the audience, ensuring that it engages with what is being said and interacts with those saying it, will help establish a good rapport quickly. This is part of the art of well-choreographed presentations. How and when to involve the audience needs careful consideration – we have already identified the value and possible pitfalls of questions taken freely throughout the process.

Take a few moments to reflect on your pitches. To what extent do you engage and involve the audience?

What other opportunities could you generate and what kind of impact might that have?

Your answers will, of course, depend on your own industry and product area. See if any of these ideas are relevant to you.

- Provide your customers with 'before' and 'after' pictures of previous work – highlight projects and cases that are relevant to them and give a few moments to consider them and ask questions. This is not just relevant to designers and those providing tangible services but also to management consultants who can present synopses of relevant case studies in a few lines – what was the problem and what was the outcome?
- Are there any tangible items for people to examine? Models, samples of materials, colour charts or indeed the product itself. Nothing beats feeling the quality or seeing the workmanship for yourself. Physical evidence is very powerful in influencing customer perceptions. Even better if you can leave examples behind – they act as a reminder of what you had to say, a good example of impact.
- If demonstrating how something works – perhaps a piece of software or a new gadget – consider whether you can let one of the client team do the demonstration. If you can, do take time to practise your coaching skills. You need to get the instructions across clearly because if your demonstrator fails the feeling is likely to be negative, and your product will be perceived as too hard to use or it will be seen as costly to train staff.
- Ask the audience members specific questions – what colour do they prefer, or which example would they like you to illustrate, etc. You are looking for a way of involving them in the customisation of their own solution. This could be as simple as the size and frequency of their likely order, the speed of service needed and so on. Involving them here demonstrates the flexibility and customisation of your offer – it's made to measure!
- Ask someone to describe his or her particular need or experience in this product area.
- Get the audience members to fill in a short preferences questionnaire to provide the feedback you need to put your final proposal together.

Involving the client takes skill but it certainly adds impact. If it is not something you do already then try it a little at a time – build your own confidence in being able to maintain control.

Presenting complex data

My first challenge to you would be 'do you have to?' A lot of complex data is about the technology of the product, how it is made and how it works, rather than the benefits it offers. The problem with complex material is that:

- not everyone in the audience may have the knowledge to understand it;
- it often needs time to absorb and understand;
- it is a catalyst for complex questions which those pitching may not be able to answer – or at least answer on the spot;
- it can break up the flow of a presentation;
- comparing complex data between competing pitches is often difficult because variables may be defined differently.

There are options open to you. For example, you can highlight key findings or the characteristics implicit in the complex data – in doing so remember to focus on what this means to the client.

If you find this difficult ask yourself the 'so what' question. 'So, what' does this mean or do for the customer. Remember the features into benefits discipline we looked at earlier.

Alternatively you can simplify complex data. Round numbers up or down, use pictorial presentation, bar charts or pie diagrams. You could develop and populate process maps if the listener is likely to find it difficult to visualise what is happening where or when.

Remember to keep thinking about engaging the audience and the impact of your message. A two-minute video clip of the production process or the product being tested may help make a complex explanation much easier to understand. With today's technology this does not necessarily need five-star production values to be perfectly acceptable.

You could produce different versions of technical documents – one set for the technical experts and a headline set for others. Offer these to the audience, or consider:

- sending them in advance for review;
- leaving them behind for analysis after the pitch.

Your decision depends on the purpose of the pitch and the expected timings of decision making as well as the nature of the data being presented.

If the customers are not experts and it is likely that they will need to compare technical aspects of competitive products then help them. Your understanding of their problem with evaluation is further evidence of your empathy, and the fact you are suggesting and supporting such comparisons signals your confidence in your offer.

Again there are options for your approach.

- **Perhaps the comparison has been done by an objective third party – the equivalent of *Which?* magazine in the consumer markets.**
- **You can identify the key characteristics for comparison and fill in the results**

for your own offer and those of the key competitors – do keep this truthful and honest. You can, however, influence perceptions by the factors highlighted or those that appear near the top of a list. For some reason, people tend to assume that items at the top of a list are more important than those at the bottom – of course, this is not necessarily true.

- You can simply provide customers with a list of the things they would be advised to consider when comparing competitive offers.

If you take this last approach do make sure to define terms for the customer and highlight any tricks of the trade or differences in presenting product data. For example:

- prices may be quoted ex VAT, or insurance or delivery, by some suppliers;
- prices could be per pack (and different sizes are used) rather than per treatment or litre;
- service contracts may be inclusive or extra;
- the product may come in different quality levels or have differences in functionality.

Only if you help the customer like this can you be sure that you are competing on a level playing field.

Adding the price tag

Price is a potential barrier to any sale. Individuals and organisations have limited resources and plenty of competing needs, so saying 'no' because of price is not the same thing as saying 'your price is too high'.

Understand opportunity cost

If your customer has not already decided to make a purchase you need to take account of opportunity cost.

It is important to try to establish where the customer is in terms of the decision-making process before you pitch. There is a difference between:

- **pitching the benefits of outsourcing the customer's call centre activities;**
- **pitching the benefits of our call centre services compared with others.**

Opportunity cost is the cost expressed in terms of the lost benefits that would have flowed from a different choice. For example:

- the cost of a new car is the loss of the tan and relaxation, fun and new friends you would have made if you had taken the two-week Caribbean cruise instead;

- the cost of outsourcing your call centre is the loss of direct control, flexible response and company knowledge which characterises your in-house operation.

Once you understand the opportunity cost decision you can use it to help make your pitch.

- 'The cost of the holiday is the loss of stress-free motoring for 52 weeks, the increased worry about family safety in an old car, the loss of any residual value.'
- 'The cost of your in-house team is the management time involved in recruitment selection, the lack of flexibility in meeting demand peaks and the wasted costs in troughs, etc.'

What is the price?

Even fairly simple purchase examples can have quite complex answers when you address the question 'what is the price?' Think about buying a new car. Is the real price:

- the list price promoted in the windscreen on the dealer's forecourt?
- a specially reduced price to encourage a quick decision?
- the cost after you have factored in the cost of financing?
- the cost including running costs and maintenance?
- the cost of the above but minus the residual value after three years or so?

The customer may be presented with only the price at the top of this list but their decision will factor in all the other dimensions. The question for the sales presenter to consider is should they ignore that or address it directly and help the customer compare the different costs.

You can use scenarios or case studies to help to illustrate your points and to add realism to your information. Suppose a customer bought a similar model for £30 000 over three years. His costs were:

		£
Car cost		**30 000**
Finance cost		**3 500**
Maintenance		**1 500**
Running costs (10 000 miles p.a.)		**10 000**
Total		**45 000**
Car's residual value	**–**	**20 000**
Total	**=**	**£25 000 over 3 years**

Equivalent to £160 for a week's motoring or £0.83 a mile travelled.

By expressing the cost per day – or use, serving or square foot of space – you make the price seem more affordable and so help to reduce the price barrier.

You might also help the customer to compare this cost against the other options.

In many scenarios, particularly business-to-business markets, there is no single list price. Rather, the price is based on the specifications of the order – the selected variables and any additions the customer chooses. The offer is essentially a menu and the various items in it have a price.

This menu may be à la carte or table d'hôte with a set meal and a choice of added extras. In this case price cannot be presented until the customer's order is specified. You can however:

- give some examples of what previous clients have spent – this gives the customer a 'ball park' figure;
- offer a range of average industry prices – for example, a new build without land costs might be between £100 and £130 a square metre;
- a silver-level package would cost an estimated £*x*, the gold option £*y*.

Do take care if adopting this approach. It can be tempting to present a price lower than it is likely to be. The problem is that you are setting up customer expectations. Overpromising and underdelivering is the kiss of death to any long-term relationship. So choose realistic prices and examples that reflect a higher and lower price point.

Watching body language

As your presentation progresses it is vitally important to keep an eye on the body language. Remember that delivering the pitch is of little value unless you take the audience with you! Look out for signs of:

- support and agreement;
- confusion or disagreement;
- boredom and lack of interest;
- disagreement within the client team.

If you have supporters and dissenters, don't be tempted to keep wooing your fans – they are on your side already. Focus your efforts at helping sway the 'not-sures'.

When you hear body language, do not ignore it – address the issues.

- Check if the audience has understood the point – ask if further clarification is necessary.
- Take action to re-engage the disinterested. Focus specifically on what it means for them or their area.
- Ask a direct question of those people in terms of what they would like to see or would be concerned about.
- Stop and give the client a chance to ask questions.

- Capitalise on the identified support – '... is that something you have experienced.'

Tackling questions

Whatever the questions, welcome them. They are evidence that the client is engaging with you and what you are saying, and this is a good sign.

If a relationship is going to be based on dialogue then you need to get used to answering questions – and you can't expect them always to be easy.

Decide on your question-answering strategy in advance. That entails not just when you want to take questions but who answers them. A really well-balanced presentation, where everyone played a part, can be overshadowed if only one team member can or does tackle the questions. So decide who is answering on what topics or issues. Reassure more inexperienced staff that they can always open up the question to other team members if needed.

Having a chairperson helps when it comes to questions because he or she can:

- seek clarification of the question to ensure that it is understood;
- field the question to named team members based on what has been asked and by whom.

Avoid the politician's answer. Nothing can damage perceptions of trust, honesty and openness more than the 'avoiding the question' technique perfected by many politicians.

Read this exchange between a potential client (C) and a sales team (T) pitching for the sale of new machinery.

C – Are your repair costs higher than the competitor's?
T – In tests our product has been shown to be equal or better in terms of reliability when compared.
C – Yes, but what about repair costs?
T – We have a robust approach to repair contracts. A service level agreement would be established to meet the needs of your business.
C – Yes, but the cost?
T – Recent research among our customers gave us an above-average rating when it came to value for money for our repair service.

- **How would you feel if you were the customer?** It is much more impressive to answer the questions asked directly and honestly.
- **Answer first and justify after** – 'Our repair costs are an average of 10% higher than those of the competitor. However, our reliability ratings are *y*% better, reducing the need for frequent repairs. We find annual repair costs per machine are equal to or just below those of all our key competitors.'

Don't be surprised

What do you do about those questions you just don't know the answers to? You will get them, so don't be too surprised. First of all remember that you are not expected to be the font of all knowledge – you represent the organisation but don't embody its collective understanding, experience and wisdom. Then:

- be open – admit you don't think you can answer the question;
- clarify why it is important to the customers – if you know why they need an answer you may be able to help with another piece of information;
- agree with the clients on how you will get the answer to them:
  - in writing;
  - by getting your expert to call their expert;
  - in the proposal.

Then make sure this happens. Follow up on the action and make a point of checking with the client that it answered the query and that there are no follow-up questions.

Remember that questions give you clues – clues about concerns and possible objections. Listen carefully and try to put yourself in the questioner's shoes. What lies behind it? Can you not just give an answer but also add the reassurance? To do this you may need to ask a few probing questions of your own.

Let us revisit our machine sales team to illustrate the point.

HR director – I understand this machine works in a similar way to that other machine. What is its safety record?

Sales – Have you had a safety problem with the other machine yourself?

HR director – We have had problems with guard rails and poor procedures followed by the operators because of the time taken to set the rails up.

Sales (now the seller knows the issue more precisely) – Well, the technology of this machine is similar but the guard rail issue was one that featured in the product development. A new alarmed system is a feature – if the rail isn't locked in place the alarm is activated. Setting the rails now takes 15 seconds, rather less than the average two minutes for the other machine. Training for the new machine takes about two hours for an experienced operator and so far no health or safety incidents, from some 150 clients, have been reported. I can put you in contact with the HR director at ABC Ltd if you want feedback from her.

So, how would you feel if you were the HR director – reassured?

It's a question of money

What do you do when faced with the budget question? We love it but can't afford it. First of all you need to assess whether this is a way of opening a negotiation on price. In which case the client is actually saying – we like it and want to see how good a deal we can get.

You should be prepared for negotiations. You need to know what is valuable to the client and cheap for you. If you can't move on price then say so clearly, but focus on the benefits you can add to the package – free training or a first-year service contract. If you can negotiate, do so but carefully. Remember the price you use to win the business will be the price clients expect you to better when it comes to repeat business.

Clients may actually have budget constraints. If this is the case you need to help them to work within these if you want the business. This can be offered in a number of ways.

- Help with financing, credit terms or payment in stages – for example, capital costs spread over two financial years may make the deal possible.
- Scalability – they could start with the basic model and extend take up as budget becomes available.
- Reduce the ingredients – we could do it for £*x* but without these features.
- Perhaps you could help the buyer make the business case for a bigger budget – perhaps the sale cost is higher but the running costs or cost of ownership is lower.

Remember – a strong finish

You have already considered the importance of first impressions – well, those final images linger as well.

Make sure your finish is as strong as the start. Try to avoid questions petering out, the clients shuffling off and a rather feeble 'well if that's all then' hanging in the air. Maintain the pace to the end but don't keep pushing for questions that aren't there.

- Make a point of being aware of the time. For example, saying 'We only have a few minutes left but do you have any questions' is a simple device but it reassures clients that you haven't forgotten the time.
- Summarise – be succinct; tell them what you told them; highlight the benefits and focus on issues which came up as possible obstacles during questions.
- Agree the next steps. Ask about their timetable, what they might need from you and confirm any follow-up information you will be sending.
- Issue any leave-behind information or remind people of the information you have already given them and what it covers.

- Finally focus on the client, not your presentation kit, as you say goodbye. Firm handshakes, smiles and eye contact are again the order of the day.
- Ask for a few moments to collect your belongings and equipment and make a tidy exit.

Adopt this approach and you should be leaving behind an impression of professionalism, competence, approachability and openness.

About that impact

The impression you leave may be positive but you want to be sure it's memorable. We have considered the importance of impact throughout. We are trying to answer the 'why should they remember us' question.

It can be little things like the matching corporate tee shirts that the team wore, or the video demonstration and hands-on session with the equipment that everyone had. It could be the leave-behind gifts or the fact that the MD met the customer at your front door and joined you for refreshments.

Take care it isn't too gimmicky but do give impact some thought. Here are a few ideas:

- The MD may not be available in person but a personal note thanking the client for the opportunity to pitch may be appropriate – or how about a video clip of the MD reassuring the client that your promises will be honoured and delivered?
- Look for personalisation opportunities. Add the client's logo to your paperwork and put individual's names on leave-behinds, but remember to have spares for latecomers and substitutes. Have that welcome sign in reception and book reserved car spaces.
- Remember the impact of engagement and maximise the opportunities for touching, feeling and seeing your business in action.
- Bring a satisfied customer, or at least endorsement video or hard copy reference, with you.
- Make sure your content has impact – use humour, or at least interesting headlines.
- Show people, don't just tell them. A picture is worth a thousand words – so use your time with clients to help them really get the picture.

You slip on banana skins!

Humour can work, it relieves tension but it has to be well executed to be effective. Don't add humour for its own sake or try turning the straight man into a comedian. Take particular care that no offence is given – avoid jokes based on sex, race, age, politics and religion. In international markets humour can be very different so it is probably best avoided – many cultures find the cynicism and sarcasm of British humour hard to understand.

Next steps

So impact matters and if you pitch with punch it will help you to win more business.

Take your time to review your current approach and performance against the ideas suggested here. You will already be doing much right but identify areas of improvement and prioritise these. Look for the high-impact and easy-to-do things so that you can enjoy some quick wins.

If you are pitching frequently make sure that you create checklists to help avoid mistakes and ensure everyone knows his or her part and has all the necessary kit.

Answers: What an impression

1 Well intentioned perhaps but this is a catalogue of errors. Gifts in multiples of four or nine are considered unlucky. They should be formally presented – handed with both hands at the *end* of the meeting to the most senior person. In Japan the *ceremony* of gift-giving is as important as the gift.

2 This is acceptable – gifts to celebrate and say thank you and which can be shared by all are particularly acceptable. If you had bought them a new office clock then the omens would have been bad as this is a symbol of death.

3 A good decision. Gifts are normally of high quality and exchanged only by close friends and contacts.

4 This is likely to be very embarrassing as the public sector, like most FTSE 100 companies, has very strong rules on accepting gifts – particularly with a high intrinsic value. If in doubt ask what is allowed.

5 Right idea, wrong number and flower. Roses are romantic symbols and flowers in Italy should be given in even numbers but never 6 or 12.

Answers: How do you want them to feel?

You may have different ideas but even so you should realise that you have a different set of 'outcomes' you want to achieve at different stages in the pitching process. Once you have a sense of how you want people to feel, you can consider what actions you can take to encourage those responses.

Phase	*Time into presentation*	*Feelings established*
First impressions	0–10	◆ Professional ◆ Friendly ◆ Approachable ◆ Organised
The presentation	11–40	◆ Relevant ◆ Confident ◆ Expert/knowledgeable ◆ Reliable ◆ Experienced ◆ Structured ◆ Empathetic
Questions and answers	41–55	◆ Attentive ◆ Honest/trustworthy ◆ Straightforward ◆ Knowledgeable ◆ Capable ◆ Focused
Closing	56–60	◆ Responsive ◆ Different ◆ Right for the job

winning proposals

What are they?

Proposals are written documents which specify how you will tackle customers' problems and satisfy their needs. What goes into a proposal depends on the context. Proposals can be part of a tender document, left after a pitch, developed as a result of becoming the chosen supplier or in response to a more informally issued brief.

This chapter examines:

- the various elements that go into a proposal – the DNA;
- what should be included and what excluded;
- how to structure a winning proposal;
- the difference between written and spoken approaches to winning business;
- how to add impact and sales messages in a proposal;
- the legal considerations of proposals.

The problem with proposals

Pitches and presentations involve face-to-face interactions. You can see if clients agree with you, test their understanding and answer their questions. Proposals have to stand on their own. They may not be supported by a presentation and even if they are, they will be read and reviewed without the supplier present.

Because of this, clarity is crucial. When developing a proposal you need to think about:

- structure;
- simplicity of language;
- navigation – to help the reader through the materials;
- how to ensure its messages are succinct.

On top of this you also often face the challenge of ensuring that your approach is differentiated from those of competitors, so your brand and corporate personality must be evident and you need to embed selling messages carefully in the document. Therefore, it isn't surprising that designing effective proposals takes time and a lot of thought.

Besides the fact that your proposals must stand alone, they also need care because they can form part of the legal contract. This is a step further than saying you need to manage customer expectations. Your proposals will often be explicit in stating what you will do, by when and for how much. It is therefore important that the legal implications of your proposals are understood by the team developing them and that detailed work on costings and schedules are completed carefully, or that caveats are clearly added to the proposals.

The written format is often more difficult to manage. As we increasingly work online with e-mail, conference calls and mobile phones, the skills of mastering the written word are diminishing and you may need to provide training to one or more of your team to ensure that your written proposals do justice to the quality of your product and service.

Proposals as physical evidence

Long after the memory of a well-executed presentation has faded, the proposal that resulted from it may sit in someone's filing cabinet – physical evidence of how your team delivers its client services. You have already considered how physical evidence can add impact to a presentation. In this chapter we need to consider the physical evidence of the proposal documentation.

Find two or three recent proposals presented by you or your team.

Try to put yourself in the customer's shoes as you take a dispassionate look at the documents. Don't concern yourself with *what* the proposals say but *how* it is said. This time the quality of your paper, the typeface selected and the layout are the 'body language' which gives clues about your culture and approach.

Use the matrix below to help you review the physical evidence of your proposals. Identify the 'good' and the 'could be better' characteristics. While undertaking your review consider how the two or three examples compare with each other. Are they clearly from the same business? Or are your proposals developed in an ad hoc way, the style and layout depending on who the author is?

	Good things	*Could be better*
First impressions – look and feel		
Structure and ease of navigation		
Brand and personality		
Reader friendliness, volume of material, visuals, summaries and white space		

You might also look at proposals that your organisation has received from others. What can you learn from these?

If you find it hard to locate any written proposals then you need to consider carefully why this is. Internal business teams are often very bad at following the formal brief to proposal process. The result is frequent misunderstanding and work being redone by internal teams. If this characterises your team I recommend that you adopt a more formal approach. Try doing this on a pilot basis and assess if it helps to improve the performance and profile of your department.

Start with the brief

Proposals are sent in response to a brief. The brief spells out the client's need and the services required from you. This might be specific – 'I want two new windows fitted' – or more open, requiring you to suggest a solution in response to a request – for example 'I would like to reduce our energy bill by 20%'.

The brief may come to you in many formats, each with its problems and limitations.

- An **invitation to present proposals or respond to a brief** – these approaches are less formal than a tender and are often used in the world of architecture and marketing, or issued for repeat business when the supplier is already in place. A shortlist of agencies are sent the brief and are invited to respond.
- **The tender** – a process used extensively in the public sector and by large organisations for big projects. This is a very challenging approach where what is required and the structure for presenting the information is specified. This involves extensive work and the provision of considerable documentation including, for example, company accounts and quality award certificates.

  The actual brief is part of the tendering documentation and will normally be quite specific in terms of volume, quality and the timing of work. It is usually possible to ask for clarification of the brief or additional information, but this would also be shared with others responding to the tender.

Before committing resources to responding to a tender, you should consider carefully your potential competitive advantage. If you have had little experience in these types of projects you need to think hard about the likelihood of being successful.

There may be limited opportunities to find out more about the client's business or needs and your proposals will often be judged against others.

This is really a tip for companies that use this approach to selecting suppliers. The process is unlikely to generate the best solution or outcome. So use the approach to choose a supplier – do not necessarily adopt the output presented in this first instance. When the supplier knows you and the business needs better, it may be more able to suggest a more effective customised solution for you.

- **A face-to-face briefing** – this is usually delivered by the buyer or a member of the client team with an understanding of the area. It may be a written document but is supported by discussion, questions and answers and a detailed look at the business. It could be the result of a face-to-face presentation or be held after winning a pitch to secure the business.

  This is generally a more satisfactory approach as it allows the supplier to really understand the needs of the customer.

If your face-to-face briefing does not come with a written brief, it is your responsibility to generate one. This is typical of service requests internally or with well-established suppliers. Taking time to spell out the problem and client's needs reduces the chances of misunderstanding and saves a great deal of time and energy later in the process.

Never try to develop a proposal if you are not 100% clear about what the client's needs are – always seek clarification. Don't be surprised if the briefs you receive seem inadequate. Briefing is generally not done well by business and will not usually be done by either internal business teams or by customers in domestic market settings.

If in doubt go back – in writing – to seek clarification or confirmation of the brief.

Checklist for a brief

A good brief should include the following:

- the client's background;
- its need or problem;
- the general context – size, scale, urgency, first-time buyer or replacement purchase;
- any specific outcomes required – quality standards, performance levels, etc.;
- constraints – usually this means issues of budget, time or security;
- methods of working – how the client wants to be involved in terms of decision-making protocols, frequency of meetings, etc.;
- other relevant information and background that might help – for example, previous history or experience.

As well as this the brief might include specific facts and figures for the business.

Take this basic checklist and customise it for your organisation. Use the list to check new briefs to ensure you have all the information you need before you get started.

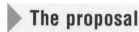

The proposal

Think of the brief as the opening round in a dialogue between buyer and seller.

- **The brief says** 'Buyer: Hello, this is who I am, this is my problem, how would you help me solve it?'
- **The proposal says** 'Seller: Pleased to meet you – this is who we are, this is how we would help you and this is why you should trust us to help you.'

It's a simple process when you put it like that, but:

- What should go into the proposal and what should you omit?
- How should you structure it to add impact?
- How do you turn it into a sales document?

The DNA of proposals

The list of possible ingredients for inclusion in a proposal is significant and includes:

- your company history;
- your client list and references;
- your team members and biographies;
- supporting materials – for example, past work;
- your understanding of the client's problem;
- the methodology you would adopt;
- your proposed approach to working together – meetings, dealing with problems;
- the costs;
- the timetable;
- an executive summary.

As you start to collect all this data and information, bear in mind the 'thud' factor. The weight of information may look forbidding rather than impressive. Your task is to give customers what they want to know and make their understanding of that as simple and as painless as possible.

Proposal pitfalls

To help identify what can go wrong with proposals, take a few minutes to consider the following questions.

1 Take another look at the list of possible contents for a proposal. Imagine the first four in the list were the first four sections of your proposal – what would be the danger?

2 Your business has been operating for a number of years and you have an impressive client list – that runs to two pages – and you are proud of all of them. What is the weakness of including this list and what might you recommend?
3 Customers like to know who they will be dealing with, so you provide full details of your team's credentials and experience. What impression might this give and what options are there?
4 Over the years you have established a simple structure for working with clients – you have a monthly site visit and give them the chance to influence decisions at set points in the project – you find it works. How would you feel if you were the customer in this instance?
5 There has been quite a debate in the company about what you should include in the company history. The MD is proud of its history and heritage and favours including background on its early beginnings. A newly appointed sales and marketing manager is recommending that you focus on current standing, future plans and views on issues like fair trade. What's your advice and why?
6 Your organisation's competitive advantage is based on a methodology – how would you illustrate this in a proposal without being too long-winded?

Check your ideas with the suggested answers at the end of the chapter.

DNA revisited

Let's take another look at the list of ingredients, but this time consider how it might be used and presented in a way which is both client focused and interesting. To do this you need to assess what the client's interests might be.

Content	*Client's interest*	*Approach*
Company history	What is the client thinking? Are you reputable and do you have a track record? Are you likely to be in business tomorrow?	Avoid the history textbook approach. If you want to promote heritage then use today to do it – for example, 'Today's strong ethical approach can be traced back to the founders 110 years ago.' Add key facts and use numbers – for example, 'We have grown fourfold over the past three years.' Be interesting – for example, 'We can trace one client back to its first order in 1906.' Choose facts likely to be of interest to the client, based on its agenda or culture. Include pictures – they demonstrate tangibility.

Content	*Client's interest*	*Approach*
Client list and references	Do you deliver what you promise – are your customers satisfied?	Again metrics add tangibility – 'Last year over 90% of our business came from repeat clients'; 'Customer satisfaction ratings were 8.8 out of 10.' Add selected previous client names with a summary of the work done. Identify one or two relevant clients who would be happy to give a verbal reference and add these – giving customers the chance to make contact makes this seem more objective. Include other badges of reliability or performance – for example, quality awards or industry accolades.
Team members and biographies	Who will be working with us? Can they do the job? Will we like them?	Add details of who's who and their role in this project. Provide pictures and some insight into their personality or approach.
Supporting materials	Have you got a relevant track record? Will we like the finished output?	Take care – this is where the 'thud' can make its appearance. In some sectors this may be easy – 'before' and 'after' shots, pictures of finished products, swatches of materials, etc. Avoid full reports and big documents, use case studies and summaries instead.
Your understanding of the client's problem	Do you really understand us and what we need? . . . after all our sector is unique.	Highlighting past relevant experience in other sectors will have helped. Restate the problem and spell out what is needed to resolve it – be as specific as possible. Use the client's terminology where possible. Play back elements of its brief – this demonstrates you were listening and are trying to respond to the client.

▶

Content	*Client's interest*	*Approach*
Methodology	Will you be thorough? Will we understand what you are doing, when and why?	This is about process not output. How do you approach the work? Make the answer to this simple, structured and as visual as possible. Show clients the stages involved. In many contexts timeframes will be important – so add a timeline. Highlight the benefits of your approach and of the client's involvement at each stage. The more clarity and structure the greater the sense of confidence, professionalism and control you communicate.
Proposed approach to working together	Will we lose control? What will we do if there is a problem?	Emphasise the client's role and choice in the level of involvement. Communication is key to successful relationships so spell out the how and when of this – meetings, progress reports, updates, etc. Refer to the requirements laid out in the brief. Anticipate problems and outline a process for resolving them. You may have a service level agreement – if so include it. Spell out who they would contact and what authority that person has. This process may include the rules for arbitration if needed.
Costs	Will it be delivered on budget? Will there be hidden extras? Will I be able to afford it?	You can either present a total price or a menu of options and prices. Whatever you do be clear and transparent. Make sure that what is included is highlighted as this will be important if competitors are judged on price as in a tender. Take particular care with the treatment of VAT – specify it is at the current rate. Are expenses and travel or delivery costs included or not? Ensure that you can recoup these if location changes.

▶

Content	*Client's interest*	*Approach*
		Make clear what is *not* included, or possible extras: ◆ additional site meetings ◆ higher specification materials ◆ extra work. Do not present this as a negative, as in 'You will be charged extra for ...', but as a positive, 'We are happy to provide the following at this fee ...' Add a date – this quote is valid until . . .
Timetable	Will it be done on time? Will you be reliable?	Metrics and references may help with this. Be specific, provide milestones and add some contingency time into your plans.
Executive summary	I haven't got time to read all this – what are the key points?	It might be useful to put this at the *front* of the proposal. It needs to highlight your competitive advantage and key selling points.

Take care with international proposals to spell out the country in which legal arbitration would take place. It can be more expensive and difficult in different countries.

Tradespeople such as builders and plumbers often complain about the extra little jobs that householders seem to find when they are on site.

Try turning this into a positive. Point out in the proposal that staff will be happy to tackle additional work, if possible, at an hourly rate of £*x*. Go one step further and ask, as part of the briefing, about extra work needed. Turn your understanding of the customer's needs and behaviours into a valuable competitive advantage.

Make sure the proposal arrives when you said it would! Consider guarantees or financial penalties for late work.

When you look at the ingredients in this way it is easy to see it as a dialogue, with your responses answering the customer's unspoken questions. A useful alternative is to include the customer's hypothetical questions as section headings for your proposal.

Structuring a winning proposal

You now have the ingredients for your proposal – but how you combine them can have a significant impact on the finished document.

A note on tenders

Tender documentation is often quite specific and leaves you little room to influence the structure of the material you send. You need to focus on the wording of your content, as discussed above, but if a set structure is given then you must stick with it. This is what the audience expects to see and deviations can be perceived as an inability to deliver what is wanted.

The completed proposal must display a number of characteristics. It should be:

- easy to follow;
- specific and clear;
- persuasive;
- directly relevant – addressing the brief.

It should tell a 'story' that starts with the problem and works through how it will be solved by you and why you should be chosen. Along the way it needs to cover how much it will cost and the timescales involved. Above all, it should identify the benefits to the client.

Building a persuasion sandwich

Remember that talking about the client is both more relevant and engaging than talking about you, so try to avoid the standard, 'Let me introduce my company as a starting point.'

If the proposal is for repeat work, or you have already been selected for the job, the company details can be included as an appendix, if at all.

Remember persuasion sandwiches – they build benefits and reasons for *why*, around the more routine details of *how*.

- **Why** – what is the problem and what benefits do you want or can you expect?
- **How** – what is our approach methodology and who is in our team?
- **Why** – the benefits of choosing us, what we can offer and the experience for you.

Consider the problem of introducing costs into the proposal. Price is often a barrier, or at least a sticking point. Many proposals ignore price until the very end, and the quote is tacked on almost as an afterthought – it isn't really justified or integrated into the proposal.

Using a persuasion sandwich approach means you take a different tack.

- **Why** – this is our team, their experience and qualifications – the benefits are less risk for you.
- **How** – this is what we do and what that team will cost you – the quote.
- **Why** – these are the benefits of using an experienced team. This may be presented in terms of speed or quality of work, or perhaps references and cases from previous clients.

A variation would be to present:

- **Why** – this is the work we will deliver.
- **How** – this is what we will do and how much that work will cost.
- **Why** – these are the benefits you will get.

Your reminder of the benefits sweetens the pill of the costs involved. You are forcing customers to consider the value for money they can expect, not just the bill they will be faced with.

A recent proposal from a landscape gardener responded directly to my brief but the estimated costs were higher than expected. A persuasion sandwich approach might have finished with some facts and figures about the impact of garden landscaping on house values – a sweetener if the cost is presented as an investment.

Restructuring your proposals

Consider the sequencing of your proposals. Use the list of ingredients and your current approach as raw materials.

Imagine you are submitting a written proposal for work in competition with two other suppliers. How would you structure your document and what would be your focus in each section?

Your approach to this will be very specific but you can compare your ideas with the suggestions given in the feedback at the end of the chapter.

The value of templates

You should take time to structure your proposals so that they make sense in terms of a consistent approach. Templates help to ensure consistency and save everyone starting from scratch for every proposal.

However, templates should only give a skeleton structure – they can have embedded fonts, heading sizes and so on ensuring that all proposals from your business look like they are from one family. What the template *shouldn't be* is an off-the-shelf document which is generic and neither customer focused nor project specific.

You can help to reduce the time spent writing proposals by adding prompts to your template to remind the writer of the focus, giving lists, for example, of past clients and work summaries.

Notice the sales messages

As you make the client the focus of your proposal, so you are building implicit messages about your client empathy and orientation and this can have real impact. You are building reasons for the client to say 'yes' into the fabric of the proposal.

Think about the building firm quoting for a house extension. What can they do to add sales messages and differentiations into their proposal?

Well, think about their methodology – not just the technical approach but the stuff that might really matter to the householder.

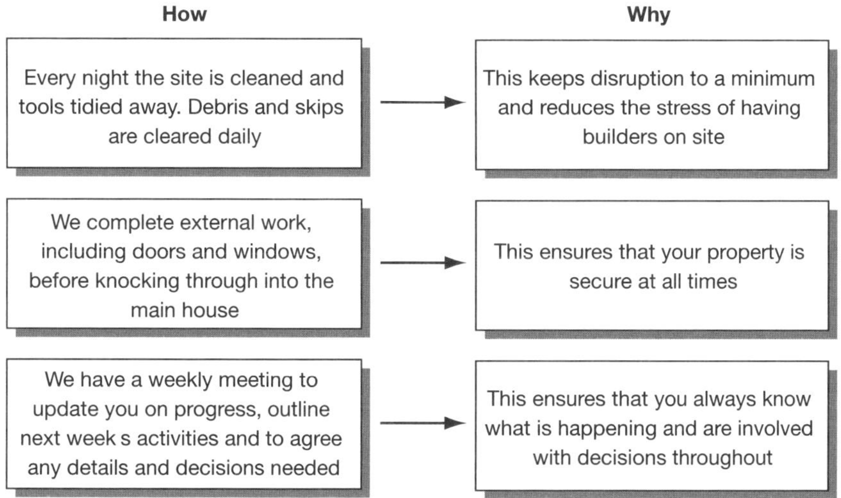

How
Why
Every night the site is cleaned and tools tidied away. Debris and skips are cleared daily
This keeps disruption to a minimum and reduces the stress of having builders on site
We complete external work, including doors and windows, before knocking through into the main house
This ensures that your property is secure at all times
We have a weekly meeting to update you on progress, outline next week s activities and to agree any details and decisions needed
This ensures that you always know what is happening and are involved with decisions throughout

Many of the competitors for this work may operate in the same way, but by being specific you are demonstrating empathy – *you know* what worries your customers so address those worries directly and turn good practice into a competitive advantage.

Brainstorm the worries your clients might have and consider how you might use proposals to address them.

In my business I know that the learning and development professions are worried about:

- the transfer of learning;
- measuring the return on investment in learning.

By addressing these two issues specifically, they recognise that I understand their agenda and this gives them confidence that I know what I am doing.

With consultancy projects, my clients are more concerned with:

- the practicality of recommendations;
- the management of specific outcomes.

In reality, in today's competitive markets there is little real difference between what one organisation and another have to offer. The real differentiators are not what you do but how you do it. These customer-focused messages highlighting the benefits from the customer's perspective make a great deal of difference.

Written not spoken

Proposals are usually written documents. Spelling, grammar and sentence structure do matter. Here are some general rules for helping to improve the quality of your written documents.

- Avoid the 'wall' of words – type which is too small and not segmented into paragraphs is very off-putting. Try to aim for at least 25% white space on the page. Use indented bullet points and space between titles and tables, etc.
- Use colour to add impact and to draw the reader's attention to key words or points.
- Add diagrams, models and pictures to break text up.
- Use headings and subheadings and make sure that they help the reader to navigate the text.
- Keep sentences short and to the point.
- The formality of your language should reflect the culture of the business. An informal style is usually acceptable but remember to add the words needed to make whole sentences – it is easy to lapse into laziness. Take care with jargon and short forms – always spell terms out in full the first time you use them.

Make sure that your proposals are read by someone else before they are sent – ideally someone who can edit the work and who will pick up mistakes, like spelling the client's name incorrectly!

Sending your proposal

You should now be about ready to send your proposal to the client. It is, of course, ready well in advance of the expected delivery date. There are still a few things that can go wrong and areas where you can demonstrate that all-important empathy.

- Ask how many copies of the proposal the client would like.
- If sending bound copies also send one unbound, or an electronic, version so

that further copies can be made easily. This is important if a proposal is to be reviewed by committee.

- Check the location and named contact for the proposal to go to. You don't want to miss the deadline because your documents were waiting for someone to come back from holiday.
- Have their arrival confirmed by a phone call or recorded delivery.
- Offer to present the proposal directly to the decision-makers.

About e-mail

These days it is very easy to send proposals and reports electronically – and there's no cost or hassle involved in physical production. This is worrying on several counts.

- You have no control over the look and feel of finished documents. They may be printed in black and white, on cheap paper and not bound. If your brand value involves quality then that quality must be apparent at every touch point. The proposal is too important as a piece of physical evidence to leave to chance.
- The client may not print off a copy of your proposal at all. Reading on screen is slow, and indeed involves a different process compared to reading hard copy – headlines and visuals become even more important.

If at all possible send hard copy – a little extra investment is worthwhile, especially if you win more business as a result.

A legal footnote

While not a formal contract, the proposal is often included ultimately as part of the contract. The proposal is, of course, only one party's promise to the other. There will need to be negotiation and agreement before your proposal becomes the basis of the express terms of a contract. However, look at what is included in a list of express terms:

- the parties;
- the location;
- dates and times;
- the price;
- details of the performance agreed;
- an intellectual property ownership statement;
- conditions of termination – frustration or breach;
- a list of remedies;
- the choice of law applicable (in the event of disputes).

You can see why care and clarity are important in developing a proposal.

If subsequently there are modifications to your proposal ensure these are recorded in writing and attached to any contracts.

If you are in doubt about the legal implications of your proposals, check it out.

Answers: Proposal pitfalls

1 All four are about your company – the customers really want to hear about their problems and your solutions to them. This content may be valid and essential, but it needs to be presented in a way that is relevant to the client.

2 More about you, not them! A long list of client names may be impressive but is not very inspiring and will have limited impact. Much better to select half a dozen relevant names in terms of sector or type of problem, with a few words about what you did and why. For even more impact add some measures of success – £*x* under budget, or resulting in cost reduction of £*z*. You can still indicate the extent of your client list in a summary statement – over three years we have delivered *x* projects for organisations as varied as W and Z.

3 It doesn't help them to 'know' the team. Add pictures and perhaps liven up the technical credentials with a fun fact, pet hate or hobby, favourite author or music. You want to give your people personality, and they need to reflect your brand values and culture.

4 An opportunity to contribute is welcome, but many would feel put out by this approach. The client will want to be consulted, or given a choice in its level of involvement. By all means identify a suggested option but provide room for modification – even if this is at a price.

5 I would support the new sales and marketing manager. Today and tomorrow are likely to be much more relevant to the client than yesterday.

6 How about a flow diagram, or similar visual tool, with arrows indicating the sequence and the benefits?

Feedback: Restructuring your proposals

There is obviously no universally correct approach to this. What is important is that you are thinking about the impact your proposal makes and how things like sequence can influence perceptions. This is a sequence that could be used.

Content	*Focus and comment*
About the clients' problem – their background and issues	Start by talking about them, not you. If relevant, include the industry context and the benefits they are looking for.
About us	This is why you are a good choice for this work – your industry experience and track record. The benefits of low risk, certainty, confidence in you.
Methodology	This is the approach you would take to tackling the clients' project/problem. Highlight the benefits of this methodology or approach.
The team	This is who your team members are, their experience and credentials.
The budget	This is what it will cost.
The outcomes and timings	This is what the clients will get for their money – benefits and standards of outputs, including a timetable.
How we would work together	Your approach to working together and the benefits of this.
Client list, references and past work	This is the evidence that you deliver what you claim to.

Development for an in-company training programme might look like this.

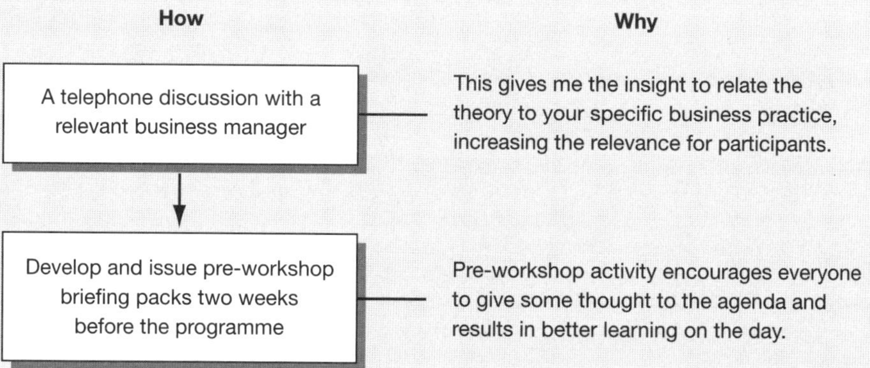

The intention is to keep clients at the heart of everything – their problem and how what you do will benefit them.

preparing to present

Communicating

Presentations, like pitches, involve face-to-face communication. Many of the skills and disciplines needed to make a good pitch will be relevant to the presentation, but in this chapter you will have the opportunity to focus on the differences and review the basic guidelines.

This chapter examines:

- the difference between pitches and presentations;
- a critique of different presentation occasions;
- a review of the importance of scoping the presentation thoroughly;
- a number of different presentation strategies and room layout;
- how best to structure your materials;
- the pros and cons of different technologies when giving presentations;
- an audit of your own strengths and weaknesses as a presenter.

Pitching – selling

You will, by now, appreciate that the terms 'pitching' and 'presenting' get used interchangeably by many client-facing teams. Whatever terminology is used, there is a difference in purpose which must be appreciated when it comes to preparation.

The presentation does, of course, have some similarities with the pitch:

- both provide a face-to-face communication opportunity;
- both involve an audience with expectations;
- in both cases that audience represents a current or potential client – be they internal or external;
- to be successful you need to plan, structure and practise both;
- the need to impress the audience with your potential or output is key to a continuing relationship.

The difference is the lack of overt selling – presentations can be defined as pitches minus a lot of the direct sell effort (see the sliding scale opposite). This difference makes the purpose, preparation and delivery of a presentation considerably different.

In a pitch the main goal is to win work; in a presentation the potential for work is a secondary goal.

Having made this distinction, it is important to emphasise the importance of always giving your best performance – the audience will judge your capability and future value by how well you deliver the material you are presenting and how good that material is.

 Scoping your presentation

No preparation can begin until you have clarified the main objectives and purpose of the presentation – if you have located yourself on the sliding scale then you can perhaps say that this is 80% selling and 20% presenting information, or whatever.

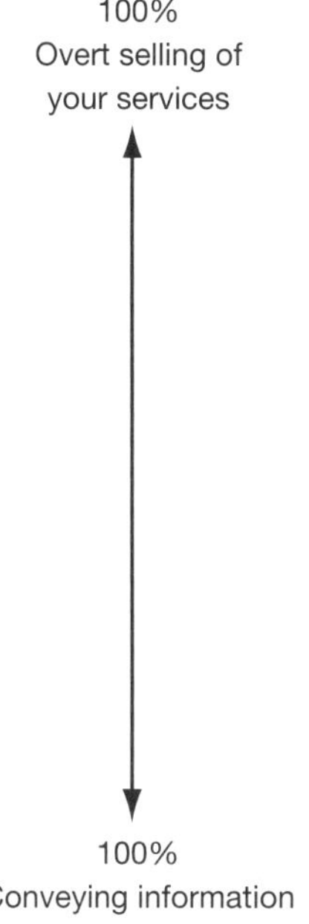

The sales pitch
You are presenting your organisation or offer in competition with others.

The sales presentation
You are presenting your capabilities, past work, etc. in a context with little direct competition – for example, internal service providers, or with a view to being added to a tender list.

Presenting in a non-client context
For example, presenting a conference paper – the audience may be future clients.

The presentation of output, information, results, etc.
This may be partway through or at the end of a piece of work.

Notice the difference?

Look at these pairs of scenarios. Which is at the sales end and which at the information transfer end of the spectrum? How would you recognise which was which if you were reviewing the scripts for each?

1a	As part of the strategy to attract clients to your stand at an industry exhibition, you are making four presentations a day on the latest technology changes in the sector.
1b	You have been invited to make a key note address at an industry conference on the technology of the future.
2a	The finance team in your organisation has an annual 'away day' for about 400 people. This year, as part of its drive to improve customer focus, it has asked you to present on finance – a customer's perspective.
2b	Your team is responsible for the organisation's facilities. You are due to present to each of the business areas on how the organisation can reduce its energy and resource use.

▶

3a	Your company has worked with this client for years. As in the past you have been invited to present your proposals for achieving next year's planned objectives.
3b	This customer has contacted you with a very open enquiry. She may in the future be interested in having some work done and wonders if you could present some ideas of what others have done in the past.
4a	You are head of a research agency who has completed a piece of market research for this client and are now presenting the findings to the client.
4b	As the head of HR you have to present the findings of the annual staff survey to senior management.

You can compare your decisions with the feedback at the end of the chapter.

Do your research

You need to start by talking to the client or organiser and answering a range of questions, as you did when planning to pitch.

The checklist below will help you to ask the right questions.

- Who will be in the audience? You need names, roles and numbers.
- What will the environment be like? Can you influence the room layout – if not what is it?
- What technology is available to you?
- Will you have technical support?
- How long will you have for your presentation? What time will it start?
- How long and under what conditions will you need to set yourself up?
- Do you know who else is presenting and when?
- Are any interruptions anticipated? For example, a chairperson who might do the introductions or handle questioning.
- Is it acceptable to give out support materials, samples, reports, etc?

If you can't find the answer to some or all of these questions then assume the worst scenario and be prepared with contingency plans for the unexpected.

When scoping your presentation you also need to create a simple brief for yourself. It should include:

- the nature of the background;
- who the audience is;
- the purpose or intended outcomes;
- how you will judge success;
- the constraints of time, resources, location, etc.

Consider the last presentation you were involved with – either as a presenter or one of the audience. Make a note of what its strengths and weaknesses were.

Even better, find a presentation being given in your own organisation by an internal or external team and try to sit in as an observer. Make a note of the strengths and weaknesses. Once you can judge others you will have a much greater insight and sensitivity to these dimensions when crafting your own presentations. What were the objectives of this presentation? Assess the balance between selling and information-giving that you would expect before they start.

	Strengths	*Weaknesses*
Organisation		
Structure		
Content		
Engagement with audience		
Handling questions		
Use of visual aids		

- To what extent were the presentation objectives achieved?
- Was the balance of selling and information-giving about what you expected?
- Make a note of two things done well in this presentation, and also two things that could have been done better.

Factors that make a difference

You have already seen that the extent of the selling element involved in a presentation is likely to influence its style, tone and content. That is not the only factor to make a difference and it is important to determine these when you scope your presentation.

Size of the audience

Audience size is another differentiator between pitches and presentations. While a pitch would be unlikely to attract an audience of more than a dozen you could find yourself presenting to an audience of 1200.

Presenting to two or three people can involve an informal, round-the-table approach. Three people can see a laptop screen, can work from a report and review documents in a board table layout.

Working like this means that the presenter sits at the board table as one of the group. This has the advantage of creating a sense of collaboration and sharing, but has the disadvantage of losing the perception of control and position of authority that is gained by standing. Make a decision as to which approach is most suitable in your context.

Presenting to between 4 and 15 people means that you will have little option but to stand. This immediately adds a sense of formality and you will need to use other strategies to create a sense of collaboration and dialogue. Strategies you might adopt include:

- allowing comments and asking for feedback and views at several points in the process;
- identifying and highlighting audience members who have contributed to your thinking or proposal in some way.

With a group of this size interaction is possible and not too difficult to manage.

Using people's names when asking for views or answering questions is a powerful technique. It also adds to the sense of dialogue and partnership. If sat at tables or an open-U or boardroom layout you can:

- **make a note of who is who during introductions – prepare a seating plan in advance that you can populate quickly and easily;**
- **consider giving everyone name cards – a piece of folded A5 card works well, but make sure that marker pens are available so you can read the names.**

If there are more than 15 in the audience then the options are more limited. You will be forced to adopt a more formal approach with the opportunities for interaction being much more limited. Questions and answers will need to be managed and you may need to use a chairperson to act as a coordinator.

However, if you have the facilities and space even a quite large audience can be organised to preserve a sense of informality and collaboration. Try using cabaret-style seating arrangements.

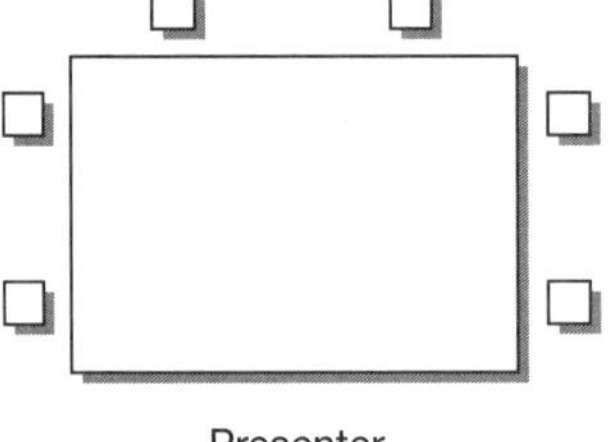

Organise the audience in groups of six or nine seated around three sides of a table – with the empty side facing the presenter.

Previewing materials, etc. can then be done by each table, each group having the opportunity for discussion amongst themselves. Feedback can be centralised from each table.

You will need to think about how you want to segment your audience – you may want to arrange tables by department or sector, interest or just randomly. Label and name the tables if the audience is segmented.

This can be a useful strategy if you are presenting to a large internal team and want them to feel part of the process. It works very well with audiences up to 60 and, at a push, up to 90.

Once you are faced with an audience above 60 it may as well be 600 or 6000. Your approach needs structure and your use of technology will be crucial. With larger audiences it is likely that you will have an event organiser along with technical backup and support. So use them – they are experts in acoustics and will know about lighting and sight lines.

Conference-style presentation preparation often assumes that the speaker will work from a lectern, centre stage. You may not have direct control over your own slides – simply a button that tells the technician to move slides. If you are not used to this style of presentation and are uncomfortable with it, ask if you can use a lapel microphone, with a waistband battery pack. This will allow you more freedom of movement. In this case, ask for a chance to rehearse if at all possible.

The audience make-up

Besides how many you need to know who to expect in your audience. Find out who is expected in terms of their:

- expertise
- roles
- area of interest/relevance of your presentation to them
- backgrounds.

Presenting to a group of experts or novices is different from presenting to a mixed ability audience.

The layout and space

You will already have some sense of how you may need to adapt your approach based on the space layout available to you.

The layout can change the atmosphere of a presentation. In my experience the limiting factor is usually space. If you have any influence over the organisation of the presentation then get involved from the earliest stage. If you don't have control, or even influence, then at least find out about the layout and develop your presentation to make the best of it. Several options are presented and discussed overleaf.

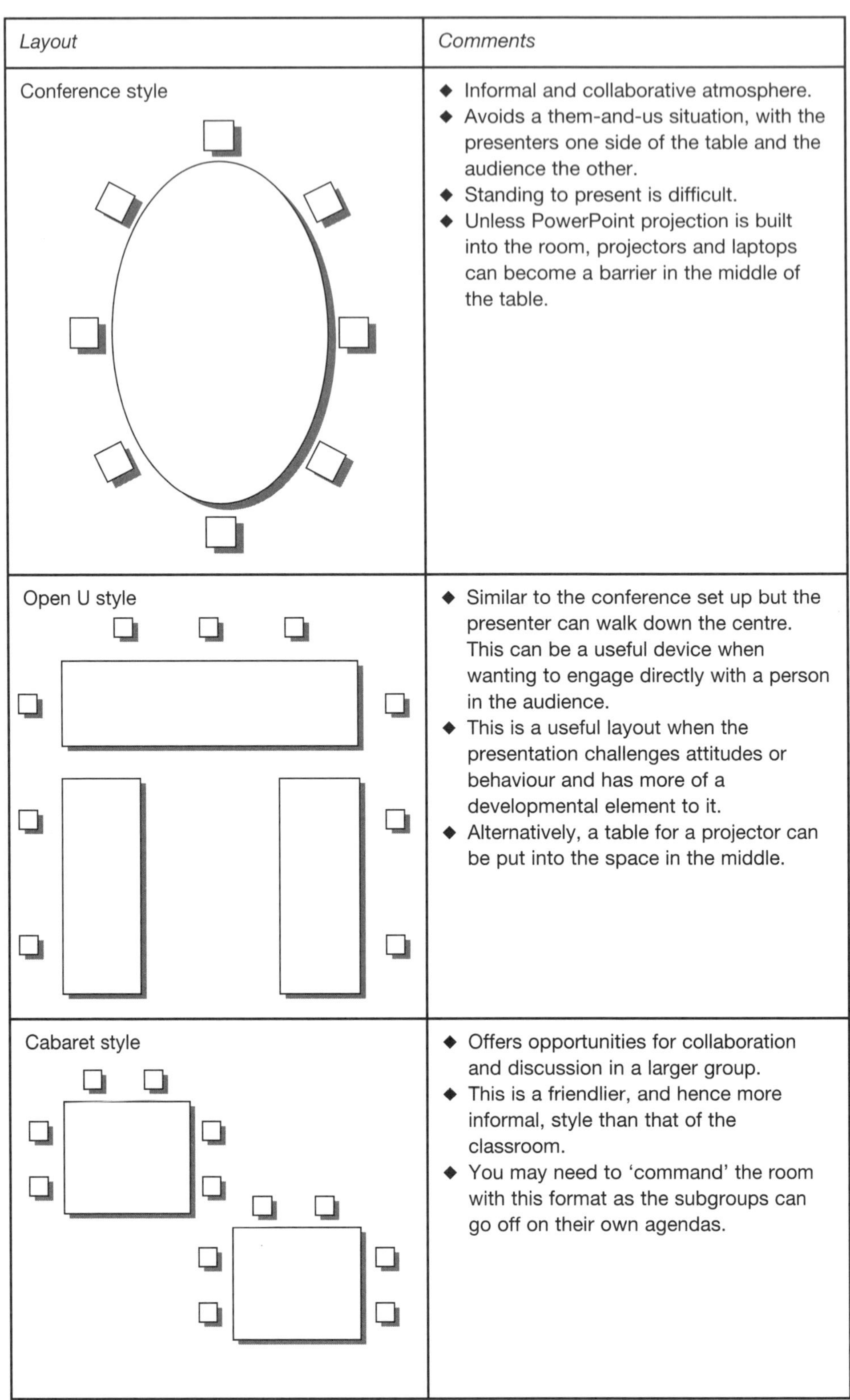

Layout	*Comments*
Conference style	◆ Informal and collaborative atmosphere. ◆ Avoids a them-and-us situation, with the presenters one side of the table and the audience the other. ◆ Standing to present is difficult. ◆ Unless PowerPoint projection is built into the room, projectors and laptops can become a barrier in the middle of the table.
Open U style	◆ Similar to the conference set up but the presenter can walk down the centre. This can be a useful device when wanting to engage directly with a person in the audience. ◆ This is a useful layout when the presentation challenges attitudes or behaviour and has more of a developmental element to it. ◆ Alternatively, a table for a projector can be put into the space in the middle.
Cabaret style	◆ Offers opportunities for collaboration and discussion in a larger group. ◆ This is a friendlier, and hence more informal, style than that of the classroom. ◆ You may need to 'command' the room with this format as the subgroups can go off on their own agendas.

Layout	Comments
Classroom style	◆ Reduces the networking and chatter you can expect with the cabaret style. ◆ Participants have desks so they can take notes, review papers, etc. easily. ◆ This is a good format if the purpose is simply to convey information.
Theatre style Tiers	◆ This is the layout used in big conferences and auditoriums – long rows of seats with no tables for writing. ◆ A good style if the purpose is to share ideas – and any detailed information is given out separately. ◆ This is a formal style that doesn't lend itself to collaboration. ◆ One advantage it has is that seating is often tiered making visibility better for a large audience.

Many in-company presentations end up using a theatre layout inappropriately. Those running 'kick-off' presentations, new product briefings and motivational sessions should avoid this if at all possible. Choose venues without fixed seating and set up a cabaret-style arrangement so that staff collaborate, network and share views and opinions. It will enhance the atmosphere considerably.

Technical resources and support

As with the pitch, the way you construct your presentation will be influenced by the technology and options for visual presentation available to you.

With large audiences and presentations, take the advice of a technician to ensure that everyone can *see* and *hear* what is going on. Check the acoustics in rooms you are unfamiliar with. Take particular care if you find yourself presenting outside as sound projection is very difficult.

Flipcharts and whiteboards are very useful when presenting to smaller groups (up to 15). They can:

- add to the sense of collaboration and involvement if everyone's views are added to a brainstorm sheet;

- help understanding if a model or approach is built up step-by-step;
- reduce the feel of stage management – the presentation evolves in real time;
- be useful when responding to questions that need explanation or elaboration.

Use *Post-it* notes and ideas or topic boards to simulate the sense of collaboration in bigger presentations. Participants can add their own comments and notes for others to share during breaks.

PowerPoint-style presentations

These are very common nowadays and are very useful. They make presentations look professional and can incorporate video clips and pictures to provide interest. They also help the presenter to keep to the presentation structure.

Conversely, 'death by PowerPoint' is a real danger and desired (or desirable) deviation from the script with its pre-planned sequence of slides can be difficult, making the presentation seem rigid and rather one-way.

If you are going to use PowerPoint then make sure you know how to use the technology. This includes linking a laptop to the projector and switching it over to projection screen mode (two monitors).

I always have a backup of my presentations on CD or memory stick as well as on my laptop. Find out in advance if projection and computers are built-in to the presentation area – if so you can usually e-mail the presentation in advance.

Video and demonstrations

These can also be very useful but again you need to have the technical support or skills to ensure they are managed effectively. Before including these in your presentation, clarify their purpose and check that they will be relevant to the whole audience.

The time factor

The final factor that will influence your presentation design is the time factor. Are you presenting in 20 minutes or two hours? You may have the choice of timings or be tightly constrained.

It is easier to prepare a longer presentation but also easier to bore or confuse the audience. Given the choice, opt for a shorter timeframe, but you will need to allow longer to prepare it.

Remember the idea of the elevator pitch (see Chapter 6). Try this with your presentation. If you had two minutes in an elevator to get your key points across, what would you say?

Selecting strategies

Once you have scoped your presentation, and considered the factors that will influence your structure, you should be well on the way to deciding your presentation strategy. This essentially establishes how you will position the presentation and this should be explicit for a team presentation. *Positioning maps* can be used to represent this strategy visually – a positioning map is simply a cross diagram on which you can plot two dimensions, or characteristics, of your presentation. In the example below, the options relate to whether:

- the main purpose is selling goods or services (as with a pitch) or sharing information (as with a presentation);
- the style should be formal or informal.

Positioning your strategy at **X** indicates a focus on selling and fairly informal style – perhaps this is a client you know well or maybe their culture is informal.

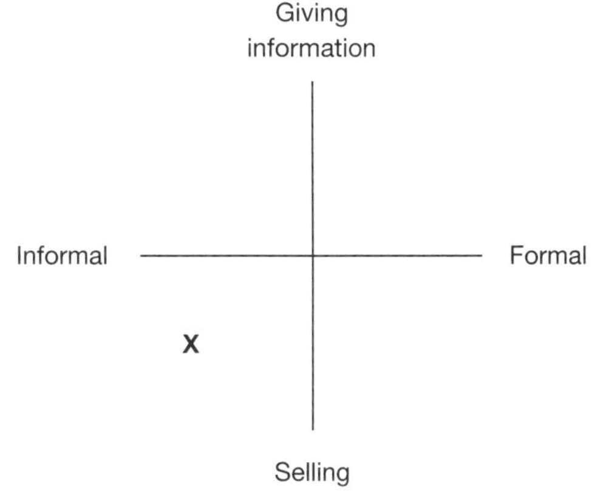

This helps the team to understand, and therefore work towards, creating a common positioning strategy – for example, the style of dress and formality of address would be clear. You can think of a positioning map as the strategist's equivalent of a blueprint.

In the next example, the presenter is trying to decide on content depth and presentation style. A cross at W implies that only headline findings will be presented and this will be done in a 'from the front' lecture style, telling the audience what it needs to know. A cross at Z also indicates keeping control from the front but would lead to better coverage of detail in the presentation. On the other hand, a cross at Y indicates getting through a similar amount of detail but involving the audience more in the process, perhaps with more questions and answers.

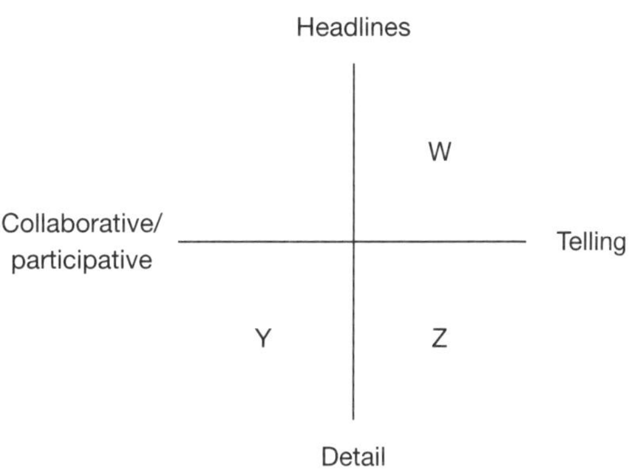

You can use positioning maps like these to help you to think about your presentation options and confirm your approach. You choose what to put on the two axes, as long as they represent an important dimension of the presentation. So a UK sales team presenting to a German client may put the English or German language on one axis. There are a number of options for your choice of dimensions shown in the illustrative maps below.

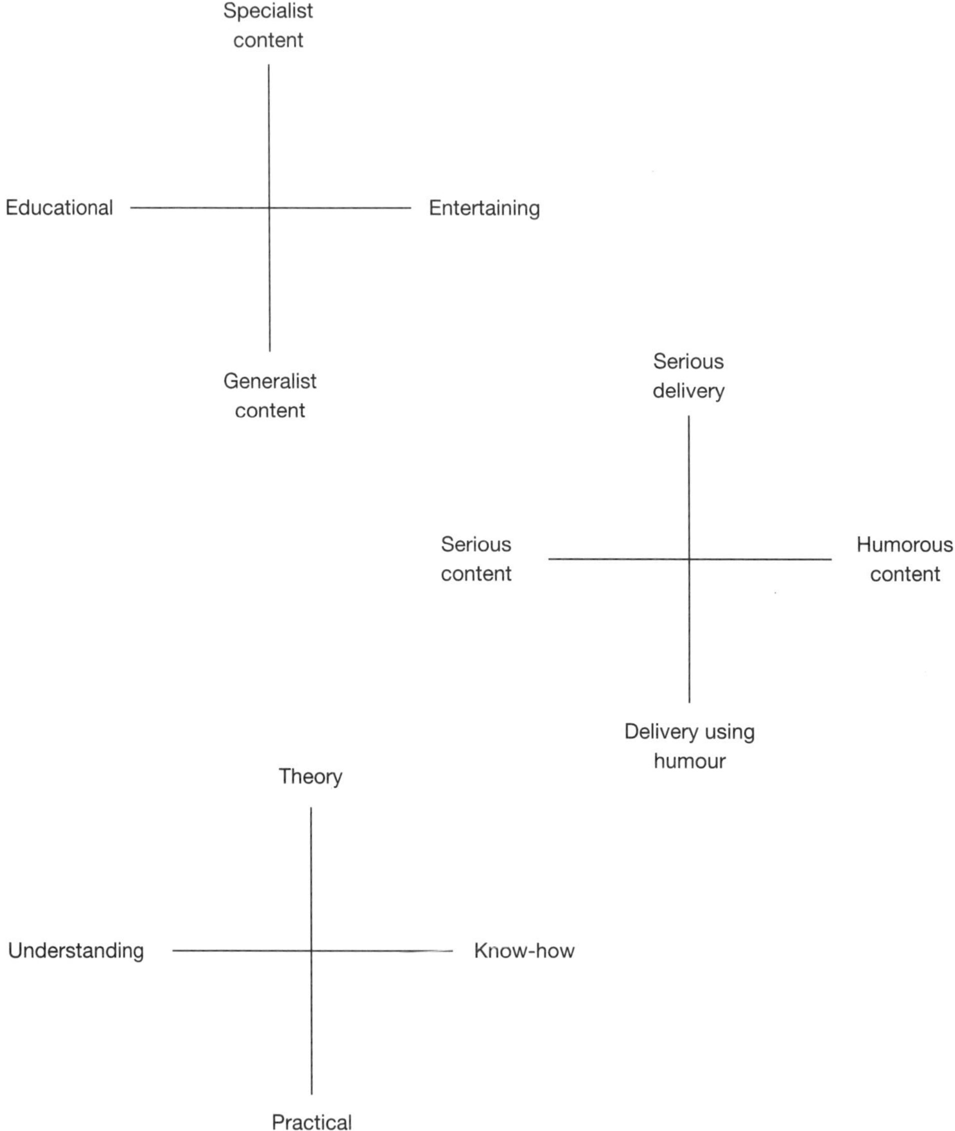

Once you have chosen the key dimensions for your presentation strategy and characterised its positioning, you can use this to check every aspect of the presentation as you develop it.

For example:

- your choice of language will need to differ if your audience is generalist rather than specialist;
- you may choose more casual dress if taking a more informal presentation approach;
- you might use formal qualifications and badges of expertise if taking a telling/expert positioning.

Understanding positioning

Look at the three alternative positioning strategies illustrated on the positioning map below. If you were asked to organise the arrangements for presentations A, B and C, describe the presentation plans you might use to support the agreed positioning – in terms of approach, layout, time and the technology you might use.

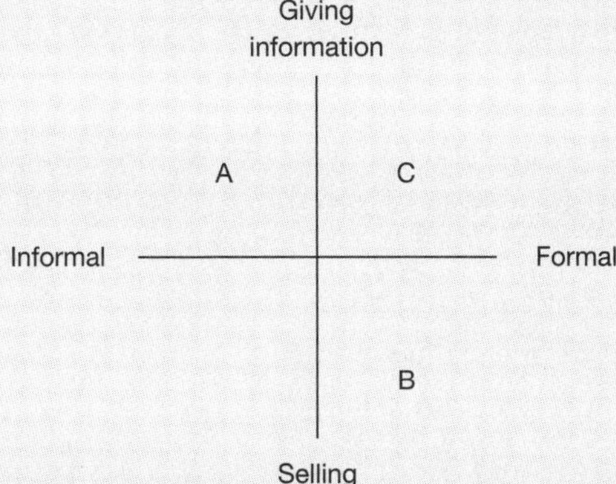

You can compare your ideas with the suggested answers at the end of the chapter.

Now – think about the last presentation you did.

- How would you position it now?
- Would any changes in your approach have helped this positioning?

Structuring presentations

You are now ready to start to structure your presentation. The biggest danger is trying to tell people too much.

- People can only absorb so much information. Attention spans are generally reckoned to be about 15 minutes concentration at a time. Then you need variation.
- The more complex the information and the less expert the audience, the less you can hope to communicate effectively. Your job as the 'expert' will often be to simplify the key data and messages.
- If you are presenting to win the work, try to avoid catalogue lists of past clients and staff qualifications – you can provide these in supporting documents.

Instead use headlines: 350 projects for blue chip clients managed over the past two years; or all our team leaders are qualified and registered by the lead professional body.

- If you are presenting on progress, it is tempting to tell your customers, chapter and verse, about what has happened since your proposal was accepted. If they trust you and have already agreed to your methodology then the most they need now is a reminder of it – so focus on what you found out or recommend rather than telling how you did the job.

That does not mean that you don't need to justify conclusions and recommendations – you do. However, the detailed data can be provided separately – you are focusing on the information.

The amount of content you can deliver will be determined to a large extent by the context and time available to you. If you are presenting a client with the outcomes of a significant project then it will expect a sense of value for money. If you are presenting a simple piece of information then you can afford to make it short and sharp.

Use a mind map

When trying to decide your content you might try using a *mind map*. This allows you to:

- capture all the content areas and points on one sheet;
- add layers of detail from each key point;
- highlight opportunities for 'soft selling'.

The mind map opposite could be used in presenting market research findings.

Once you have a mind map, you have a picture of all the content options. Now you can pick and choose what should be in and out. You can focus on headlines or add more detail. You can see the linkages between content and this will help you to structure your 'story'.

You can follow the structure in different ways round the mind map. You could follow the timeline defined by:

- the client's problem;
- our methodology;
- identifying the customers;
- deciding a methodology;
- what the findings were.

You may have more impact by telling them the end first:

- this is what our research told us;
- about your customers, who look like this;
- this is the insight it gives us to help you tackle your problem, which was . . .;
- this is who we talked to, about what;
- and this is how we came to those conclusions.

Analysing customer behaviour for a company

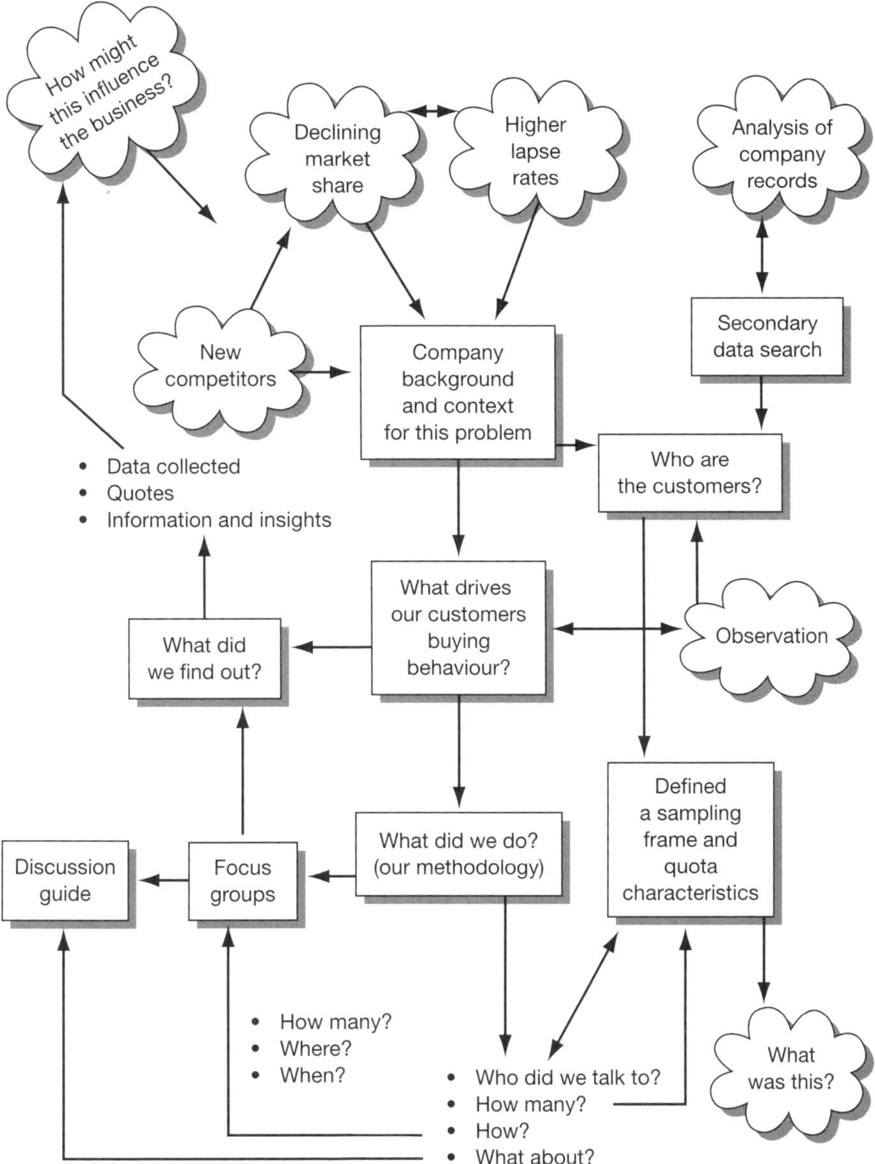

The important point is that your presentation has a logic – it tells a story that the audience can follow.

If you were doing a quick, formal, telling presentation you would stick to the main points and the timeline approach would be the most suitable.

A more collaborative style – this is what we found out, this is what it might mean – would favour tackling the findings first and adding more detail.

If you are still having trouble deciding what can be left out try using a sorting grid such as the one overleaf.

	Key information	*Supporting information*
Adds value to the audience	Priority	Add if time permits
Doesn't add much value to the audience	Provide as headlines only	Avoid

Presentations often last longer than pitches so you are quite likely to crash the 15-minute concentration barrier. You can counter this effect by varying the style, presenter or approach. Break your presentation content into pieces, and punctuate it with questions or discussion among the audience. Alternatively use a video clip or offer the chance to look at materials, prototypes or findings.

Build a presentation plan

A presentation plan is the presenter's equivalent of an orchestra score. It pulls together, on one sheet, what should be happening when. If you add a timeline to it then you can check timekeeping during your rehearsals.

The sample that follows carries on from the earlier mind map and shows how the plans for that research company might have looked.

A presentation plan

Client: ____________________ Audience number:

Location: ____________________

Timings: Start ____________________ Finish ____________________

Room layout: ____________________

Equipment needed: ____________________

Objectives:

1 ____________________

2 ____________________

3 ____________________

Time	*Plan*
0–10 min Chair	Introductions, welcome and objectives – tell them what you will tell them
11–20 min	Headlines only – the background and our response/methodology

Time	Plan
21–24 min Speaker 1 Short video clip	Your customers and video highlights from focus groups – what they were saying
25–30 min Chair	Any comments on what the customers are saying? First impressions.
31–45 min Speaker 2	The detailed findings – statistics and tables explained, key points highlighted
46–55 min	Questions
56–70min Speaker 1	So what does it all mean – summarising the insights and information
71–85 min Chair	Discussion and questions . . . what are the implications?
86–90 min Chair	Next steps – how else can we help?

As with developing pitches, you can use PowerPoint slides to help you stick to the structure, even if you only use title slides for each section.

A presentation checklist

We have already considered some of the pros and cons of slide presentations. Use the following checklist to remind you of that earlier learning and to evaluate presentations before you deliver them.

- Slide numbers – fewer is better. Never more than one per three minutes of presentation, so the 90-minute plan outlined above would have a maximum of 30 slides.
- Are the presenters adding value to the slides? The slides help by guiding your route but the detail needs adding by you. Use the 'notes' facility underneath PowerPoint slides to identify what else the speaker should say. However, if you are just going to read the slide you may as well send the presentation to the clients for them to read.
- Do the slides reflect your brand, your approach and style? As you would choose clothes to suit you, so the colours, typeface and style of graphics need to reflect your organisation.

- Check that your slides aren't too busy. Too much detail and too much movement are hard to absorb. Keep font size high, keep animation consistent and use colour to highlight key points. Generally it is better to avoid sound effects to support animation.

Invest in a remote or wireless mouse for your laptop. Nothing is worse than a presenter stuck behind the laptop every time he or she needs to access a different slide.

About support materials

When you were pitching, you had to decide on 'leave-behinds' – information about your business, samples or a proposal.

When presenting, you are more likely to leave behind business information or a report, a set of recommendations, drawings, etc. These reports and plans must be standalone documents. In other words, they must make sense to someone who hasn't seen your presentation. Relate what you say to the contents of any report by adding page references to slides, making navigation easy between the presentation and the report. Think about how best to use these materials. You have a number of choices.

- Send reports and plans in advance. This gives the audience a chance to review them and think through their ideas, questions, etc. This is a good approach if you want to create a collaborative approach.
- Give materials out at the beginning of the presentation. If you do this you should refer to the content during the presentation, perhaps highlighting appendices or specific content. There is always the danger that the audience is distracted by the report and only half-listen to what you are saying. This is not a good approach if you are presenting complex information.
- Give the materials out at the end of the presentation. This is a good approach if further contact and follow-up is planned. It gives you the chance to explain your ideas or approach, and the customer time to absorb it before the next session.

A leading research company announced, in its proposal, that it would present its findings in a 60-slide presentation. The company was unwilling to give the client access to this presentation in advance, and had no report to support or supplement it.

The impression given was poor:

- the formula of a 60-slide solution was perceived to be off-the-shelf, a fact that should have been picked up at the proposal stage;
- the lack of a written report seemed unprofessional and lazy;
- the unwillingness to let the client preview findings gave the impression that there might be something to hide.

Take care that you are giving the right impression.

Presenters and presentation skills

You have the occasion and the venue, the presentation and the supporting documents. All you need now are the people to present your plans.

Presentation skills are different, though similar, to the skills needed in pitching. In both cases you need the confidence to address a group of people, and you can't be afraid of getting up on your feet and taking centre stage.

In both cases you need not only to be up on your feet but also able to think on them. No matter how well prepared you are or how much you practise, the unexpected will always happen and you need to be able to handle that. Pitching or presenting, you are representing your organisation and new or repeat business may depend on how well you perform. It can be stressful.

Presentations are often longer, more interactive and require a deeper knowledge or understanding of the product or project. Those pitching are often selling the business and methodology whereas the presentation represents the output – it needs to be well packaged and to reassure customers that they made a good choice of supplier.

Those pitching need to be able to sell, interpret buyer behaviour and, often, negotiate deals. The presenter has much less selling to do and so more people feel comfortable with presenting than pitching – it is a less pushy challenge.

Watch out for the temptation to present when you should be pitching. This much lower-key approach to a sales opportunity may deliver a lower level of success. If you need to sell, make sure you sell!

You are more likely to find that staff who have no front-line sales role become involved in presentations to customers. They may be operational or technical staff who are involved in delivering work for the client. They may need help in polishing presentation skills and developing confidence before they are put into this role. Nerves may be understandable but they don't give the best impression. If the audience is worried that the presenter is having a tough time they won't be focused on what is being said!

Auditing presentation skills

The table overleaf represents the characteristics of an effective presenter. Use it to either audit your own skills or help to evaluate the strengths and weaknesses of others.

The best way to evaluate your own skills is to watch a video recording of a presentation.

Characteristic	*Strength*	*Weakness*
Subject knowledge, relevant experience		
Personal confidence		
Clear speaking voice, good diction		
Positive body language – open stance, etc.		
Empathy with the audience – aware of their responses		
Good eye contact		
Not easily flustered – able to cope with challenging questions		
Able to think on their feet		

Become an expert

Presentations, in their various formats, are such an important part of business today that staff with expert presentation skills are highly valued.

Take every opportunity to build your own skills as a presenter – set yourself development goals, seek feedback and opportunities to present. No matter how skilled, everyone can improve and learn from watching others.

Look for opportunities in and out of work – give speeches, coach youngsters at your sports club, or do briefings for a local charity.

Practise, practise, practise

This chapter ends with a very strong echo of the preparation for pitching. Whether the presenter is an individual or a team they need to practise. That means practise:

- setting up
- timing
- delivery
- handling questions.

Get yourself a rehearsal audience, give them appropriate roles and let them role-play their responses and questions. Try videoing this and review how you come across.

Answers: Notice the difference?

1 1a is more sales focused than 1b. I would be trying to get 40–60% sales effort into my exhibition presentations. I would want to make those sales messages implicit. For example, clearly branded examples of technology, and facts and figures or case studies that showcase the organisation's capabilities.

In 1b the sales effort may be as little as 5%. The fact that a representative of your organisation has been invited to present gives you credibility. You would want the audience to know what company you worked for and may be able to introduce a few organisation-specific comments.

2 2b has a greater sales scope than 2a. In 2b you are trying to sell the idea of behaviour changes. It will need to be filled with benefits and practical examples if you are to make an impact. In 2a you need to grab attention, perhaps making your session memorable or entertaining (away days can be very long). Unless you are championing the culture change, your role is simply the conveyor of information – what's it like to wear the customer's shoes?

3 This one is open to interpretation. I would say that 3b is more sales based and 3a more information sharing. In 3b you want to perhaps sell both the benefits of having the work done and the benefits of you doing it.

With 3a you have a relationship and there are no apparent direct competitors for this work.

4 Both are presenting research findings to their clients, so the selling element is low in both cases. In 4a you will want to ensure that the client is satisfied and is given the opportunity of future studies. In 4b the HR manager will be keen on the department being seen to be effective but the survey is likely to be its responsibility next year.

Answers: Understanding positioning

- A's strategy is based on an objective of detailed information sharing in an informal and collaborative style.

  I would expect an open-U layout for small numbers or cabaret-style for a bigger group. I would use flipcharts and *Post-it* boards to supplement key notes presented via PowerPoint. I would provide the detail in hard copy for the audience to review and comment on. It would be a long presentation.

- B's positioning is more formal and with a significant sales element – it is dealing with headlines but is telling rather than asking. This may be a commercial organisation presenting about itself to win an award or get on a tender list, or an internal team presenting already decided strategy.

  The layout could be boardroom, classroom or lecture style using a prestructured PowerPoint presentation, highlighting headlines. Questions and answers would be managed at the end of the process.

- C, like A, is presenting detailed information for sharing purposes but C is formal and telling – a university lecture or masterclass style. The different positioning would lead you to a classroom style layout with managed questions and answers ▶

at the end of the session, but still with detail provided in hard copy. A chairperson would add to the formality.

When you compare C with A you can see how the layouts and approach can change the atmosphere of a presentation. You need to manage your own strategy.

presenting with panache

It's the quality that counts

Presentation is the packaging for your project or organisation's offer. The quality of what is in your offer will be influenced by the perceptions created by how it is presented. If your service is based on quality, attention to detail or professionalism then those are the characteristics your presentation must convey.

If you have prepared well and practised there should be nothing to worry about. You will be able to approach the actual presentation focused on managing your performance and interaction with the audience.

In this chapter you will find many of the messages in Chapter 7 revisited because the basic rules are broadly the same, but we will focus on:

- how to make a strong start and good first impression;
- how to nail your nerves and help others to nail theirs;
- the importance of body language – theirs and yours;
- troubleshooting – what can go wrong and what to do about it;
- how to handle disruptions and questions;
- ways of building-in those implicit sales messages.

Expertise rather than impact

When you were pitching you were concerned with making an impact – the challenge was to differentiate you from the competition. When presenting, impact is less of a concern, the first impression you want to create is one of expertise. Your clients want to be reassured that they made the right choice, your internal customers need to be certain they can trust your judgement, and potential customers need to be convinced that you are capable of doing the work.

The challenge then is how do you create a sense of expertise and make a strong first impression? The basics are crucial.

- Arrive on time, well rehearsed and in control of the materials and technology to be used.
- Make certain everyone is well turned out – there is no need to go for the 'team look' at this stage in your relationship with the client, but appropriate dress will make an impression, or rather, inappropriate dress will make a poor impression.
- Introduce the whole team by name and individual's involvement in the project – you need to establish everyone's credentials as quickly and effectively as possible.
- If there is informal conversation before getting down to the presentation proper, focus on business rather than last night's football. Think in advance of the observations that might be interesting to the client:
  - the similarity of its project to others;
  - the particular challenges faced by the organisation;
  - developments relevant to its industry or business that has been in the news.

In order to win this work, you undertook customer research. Once you got started on the project your focus will have tended to become more specific. Before the presentation revisit the background information on the client and make certain that the whole team is aware of it, and also strategy and key industry issues.

If presenting to a domestic client or internal team then remind the presenters of the background, context and benefits needed.

- Watch the body language – your team wants to be perceived as confident and in control. Strong handshakes, eye contact and a focus on the client will all help to establish this impression.
- If you can be in the room before your audience take the opportunity. You want to welcome them to your space. If working at a board-type table do not be afraid of spreading your papers – taking up space is a strong signal of confidence and will be taken as a positive sign.
- If possible avoid barriers between you and your audience. Being 'exposed' is an invitation to trust – you have nothing to hide. This is why an open U shape or cabaret style layout can be very effective.

Nailing those nerves

Remember that nerves are not a bad thing. They improve performance as long as they are managed. Everyone suffers from the adrenaline rush that causes butterflies but uncontrolled they can lead to stage fright. You need to understand your own nerves and manage them.

It is useful to recognise the physical impact of that adrenaline in your system. As you react to stress:

- your blood pressure may rise causing a sense of panic and this can make people rush – they tend to talk more quickly, they want to get it over with as quickly as possible;

You need to make a positive effort to pace your speech. Rushed sentences do not create the impression of the confidence and control you are aiming for. It is particularly important if your audience is working in a second language.

Slow, deep breaths rather than fast, shallow ones will help counter the raised stress level.

- you get a dry mouth – so make sure that there is water available for all presenters;
- the flight or fight reaction in your body can be strong and, depending on your reaction, your body language can become more aggressive or submissive – neither is desirable so watch out for the signs and control it;

- stress can influence your body temperature, some blush, others may feel cold – do not be surprised by this, it tends to settle down as you get speaking and start to relax;
- deep breathing can help steady the nerves.

Interact with the audience before the presentation proper. You'll find that if you have greeted people, spoken to them or broken the ice in some way it helps to dissipate the nerves.

There are some simple techniques to help keep nerves in check.

- If presenting with a team, consider letting everyone say something at the outset, even if it is simply to introduce themselves and their role – having spoken prevents the escalation of stress that can result from waiting your turn.
- Give people tasks to help focus the attention of anyone suffering badly with nerves. Let them set up equipment or give out support materials.
- Try to identify what you are nervous about. If you are worried about forgetting your lines then use your slides as prompts and have key notes on cards – but use A5 card not A4 paper. Paper waves about with your shaking hands and advertises your nerves, making you feel worse and distracting the attention of the audience.

Prompt cards

Prompt cards do help – they remind you of what you are supposed to say. If you do not have the benefit of PowerPoint technology, they ensure you stick to the structure and, if you need to present detail, they ensure you get it right.

Good morning. We are here today to present to your our detailed . . .

Word-by-word prompts don't work – you'll find yourself reading

- **Welcome**
- **Why we are here**
- **What to expect**

Key points, or a sort of discussion guideline, is the correct use

Using an autocue, like newsreaders do, requires training and practice. They have the advantage of being placed in front of the speaker so it looks like they are making eye contact with the audience.

- If you are worried about handling questions then make sure you manage the timing of them and be prepared for the question that needs to be answered with, 'I don't know, but I will find out.'
- Avoid other tell-tale signs of nerves:
  - don't let presenters hold papers or documents that they might fidget with while others are talking;
  - take coins out of pockets for the same reason;
  - think about where you are putting your hands and arms – don't put them

in pockets, or fold them, both are signs of nerves, creating a barrier between you and the audience.

Supporting each other

If your team isn't interested in what you have to say, why should anyone else be? If presenting with others you need to ensure that everyone's body language is positive and supportive.

- If presenters have to sit together facing an audience – essentially on stage – then position chairs so they are off centre, aligned to face towards the speaker.
- Ensure the team is actively listening, nodding and watching the speaker. The natural tendency is to look down and seem apart from the event until it is your turn. This comes over as being disinterested.
- Link the messages of presenters positively by referring to material already presented:
  - Jay pointed out that ... following on from Sara's analysis ...
- or by promoting content yet to come:
  - 'Jay will be showing you ...'.
- Whoever introduces each speaker should again emphasise that person's role and expertise. This can be done by having different versions of a person's credentials, so it is not simply repetition. So when introducing Jay at the beginning of the presentation process I might say, 'Jay is a Masters Graduate from Cranfield who took on the role of project manager for your project.' When it is Jay's turn to speak I might say, 'I will hand over to Jay for his comments about the project management. I think you will find his experience of similar roles for organisations A, B and C makes for interesting comparisons.'

If you have recently been involved in presenting with others, take a few minutes to reflect on how well you supported each other and consider how you might do this more actively in the future.

Relate and empathise

What you say and how you say it will determine the extent to which the client engages with you. The more difficult your message the more critical it is to win that engagement. There are a number of techniques that will help – some of them have already been highlighted but we will summarise them here.

- Focus on the clients and their needs. Talk about their business, problems and opportunities and look at things from their perspective. You should demonstrate this empathy at both client level and at the level of individuals in the audience – remember the decision-making unit and their different needs and agendas.

	Commercial presentation	*Domestic presentation*	*Internal presentation*
About the client	During this time of rapid growth and global expansion your company needs . . .	Landscaping a property like this will add significantly to its value	This charge is particularly challenging for your team
Agendas of the DMU	◆ As HR director, the expanding workforce must be a challenge ◆ As MD you will be concerned with . . .	◆ As the main gardener, you will find maintenance so much easier ◆ The kids will love the safe play area	◆ As line manager, you will be worried about the effect on retention levels ◆ As shift manager, this will change . . .

Look at the above examples.

People do like others to understand things from their perspective. Your ability to integrate this sense of empathy into your presentation is very powerful.

- Acknowledge the client's contribution and input or influence on your work. This will show your partnership approach at work and provide evidence of your listening intent. So, for example: 'With the help of Neelesh in your IT team, we identified the six key causes of breakdown and lost productivity'; 'We built on Mrs. Smith's ideas for more storage and we added this window seat into the design'.

  Positioning the clients as part of the team in this way increases their ownership of the proposals and increases the likelihood of them supporting your recommendations.

- During the presentation, highlight topics that are of particular interest to a member of the audience. For example, 'John you will be particularly interested in this feature of the new machine!'
- When someone asks a question or makes a contribution listen actively. Lean forward and look at the speaker and nod if you are in agreement or to acknowledge that you have understood the question.
- Show understanding of how your proposals or product will change things for the client. It is fine to acknowledge that this will mean training or changed rotas – this is a further reflection of the cost of buying into your proposal. It is even better if you can present ideas for minimising any negative impact or costs. So, for example: 'We appreciate that this plan will involve considerable disruption but our approach will minimise this by working seven days a week and an evening shift until the changeover is complete'; 'We recognise that you will be disappointed by this result but it has also given us some insights that will help you make a real difference going forward'.

Troubleshooting

Awareness of the potential for problems represents a major step in being able to handle them. Some you may be able to avoid altogether; others you can prepare for; and those that are left won't take you by surprise. Look at the example described below and see how effective a troubleshooter you are. What are the possible trouble spots and what might you do about them?

Avoiding trouble

'Your Event' specialises in all aspects of managing company events – everything from product launches to sales conferences, from client parties to press conferences.

Six weeks ago it was delighted to win a contract for a new client, with the potential for several other significant projects if this first goes well. The client needs to host a large international conference, intended to showcase its work and future plans to over 500 key clients. Your Event's proposal was accepted.

Next week the Your Event team is presenting to a client's project team the detailed plans for:

- facilities and transport
- hospitality
- technical support for speakers
- gifts and signage.

There are five members in the Your Event team (a coordinator and a specialist for each area) and the presentation is at the client's offices in Brussels. The meeting is scheduled for 11.30 making it just possible to travel by train from London that morning, allowing for the time difference.

Your Event knows that the client has, in the past, been disappointed with logistics and the standard of catering complaining of unimaginative menus, slow registration of guests and moving people between activities and events.

The Your Event team has been told to expect an audience made up of the six people involved in assessing the pitches and proposals, plus four others including the marketing director.

The Your Event team want this presentation to reassure the client. There are many details that need to be shared and discussed but it is important not to let a series of ad hoc modifications make the overall plan unworkable.

What would you advise if you were Your Event's chief troubleshooter?

Compare your list of potential pitfalls with that given at the end of this chapter.

Troubleshooting in this way requires you to take this sort of 'helicopter view' of the key issues and again have empathy with the client.

The easiest way to prepare for possible problems is to get a small group together to brainstorm the issues that might become pitfalls. They can also usefully spend a few minutes generating a list of possible tough questions to give you the chance to prepare for them.

Tackling trouble

Your presentation will have helped you avoid possible trouble spots but there is always opportunity for the unexpected – the equipment failure, electricity blackout or sickness in your team. Some of these problems may be more likely to happen when working in overseas locations.

Scenarios and contingency planning can be useful tools to further prepare the team.

- **Contingency planning** – involves you making preparations for a possible event. For example, if you feel it is possible that the client might reduce the available budget by a third, you might have a modified plan ready that reduces the scale of the project. If you want to be prepared for presentation equipment failure, you will have available hard copies of the presentation which the audience can use.

Whether or not you usually give out copies of your presentation, it is worth having a hard copy of the thumbnails with you – this can be copied and given to the audience if needed. Take care with the number of slides you print per page. If there is a lot of detail on your slides you will only be able to print two per page.

- **Scenario planning** – involves 'what if' preparation – what if our plane is cancelled or the samples aren't ready on time? These events may be unlikely but would be significant if they did happen. Scenario planning lets you rehearse the response that you might make in such an event, and the process of doing this makes you more prepared.

You can use a simple sorting grid to help you determine which potential trouble spots to plan for and which to develop scenarios for.

		Likely to happen		
		Probable	*Possible*	*Unlikely*
Impact on your presentation	High	Plan for this and take steps to nullify the impact	Develop contingency plans	Develop scenario plans
	Medium	Plan for this and take steps to nullify the impact	Monitor for evidence of this problem	Develop scenario plans
	Low	Be aware	Be aware	Don't worry about this

Take your brainstormed list of possible problems and categorise each item in terms of:

- the likelihood of this happening;
- the impact on your presentation if it did.

Handling disruptions

'Noise' is a barrier to effective communication and noise in the form of disruption can turn any presentation into a mediocre experience. Noise is often outside the direct control of the presenters but has to be handled.

What would you do?

Look at these scenarios, each depicting an example of the type of disruption a presenter might face. What would you do?

1. Asked to present plans for a loft conversion at the client's home, the designer finds himself in a room with the TV on and the children constantly in and out.
2. During a presentation, one of your audience answers a mobile phone call.
3. The MD is called away from the presentation to handle an urgent matter.
4. There is a fire bell test.
5. There is a fire drill.
6. Two of your audience engage in a private conversation throughout the presentation.
7. Although you have asked to have questions at the end, one of the audience keeps disrupting you with questions.
8. Five minutes into your presentation there are two or three late arrivals.

The suggested answers at the end of this chapter include my thoughts on strategies for handling disruptions.

The important thing about disruptions is to *deal* with them and make a positive response.

- Do not get annoyed – the emotions involved in preparing and presenting can heighten your sensitivity to interruptions and prompt an emotional response.
- Remember your manners – if you are in the clients' space it is their rules, not yours, that are valid.
- Use breaks and recapping to help mend the flow if it gets disrupted.
- Keep smiling!

Dealing with questions

Questions come in a variety of types that people use in a range of contexts. It helps to recognise the type of question and the questioner's purpose.

Question type	*The questioner's motive*	*Your response*
Clarifying questions 'So what you are saying is . . .?'	This question is used to test their understanding.	Be clear and specific in your response. A simple 'yes' may be enough, but if it is a complex topic empathise with the questioner's uncertainty and try to offer an illustration or example. Check directly that the questioner now understands – and watch their body language. Note: frequent clarifying questions indicate that you may need to review your presentation content to see how you can simplify or clarify the key messages.
Open questions 'If it was your decision what approach would you take?'	These are used to: ◆ get more background information ◆ to establish rapport with the presentation team ◆ to establish what the presenter's views, attitudes and opinions are.	Take care not to turn your answer into a monologue. You can, for example, offer headline information and point the questioner at further sources. Avoid being sucked into giving personal rather than professional views.
Probing questions 'So what would that look like in these circumstances?'	These are a sign your audience is interested, they want to know more. Do not assume that they are simply testing or querying you. Some audience members might use probing questions to demonstrate their knowledge and understanding to their colleagues.	Field the question to the team member with the detailed knowledge to answer it. If that amount of detail is not immediately available, say so and agree when and how it might be reviewed. If necessary ask your own clarification question to ensure you understand the context that is of the most interest to the questioner.

Whatever the form of a question, do not be put off by it.

- ◆ Listen carefully to what is being asked.
- ◆ If in doubt clarify what the question means or the specific context the questioner is thinking about.
- ◆ If the question is complex break it down into smaller questions and answer each element in a logical sequence.
- ◆ Differentiate between process and recommendation questions. One asks, 'How should we tackle this?'; the other asks, 'What do you recommend that we should do?'
- ◆ Do not vacillate. Nothing is more annoying than someone who will not answer a direct question directly – it comes over as you trying to avoid the issue.
- ◆ If you cannot answer the question now, say so. Explain why you can't and then decide how, when and who will answer it.

Avoid, 'Yes .. but.'
Answers that start with a 'yes' and then add the 'but' are perceived to be the same as saying 'no'. For more positive impact try using, 'Yes ... and ...'

For example:
Question: 'I presume this budget and project plan is just for stage 1 of the work. Will there be a stage 2 and 3 with equally high price tags?'

Answer: 'Yes, this is a stage 1 plan and the benefit of breaking down the work this way means you can influence the development and spend at each stage in the process.'

- ◆ Avoid the 'weasel words'. Weasel words are used to qualify or limit the strength of your statements. Look at the following examples.

With weasle words	*Without weasle words*
On balance this is *probably* the best option for you.	This is the best option for you.
The budget *we might* need is around £35k.	The available budget needs to be £35k.
I would expect option A to *possibly* deliver more output than B.	I would expect more output from A than B.
It should be possible to evaluate the return on investment.	We can evaluate the return on investment.

Strong, clear statements come across as authoritative and confident. Weasel words signal a lack of certainty and create the query, 'If you aren't sure why would I trust your judgement?'

Handling aggressive questions

It is always possible that you will be faced with an aggressive questioner. The important thing is not to react emotionally and end up in a row.

- First, try to assess the reason for the aggression – is it culture or personality rather than a response to your presentation?
- Does the person have a cause for his or her emotional response? Do your proposals impact on his or her role or department? Empathise where this is appropriate, you could acknowledge this person's justifiable interest and concerns and negotiate his or her greater involvement in the process going forward.
- If you can't establish a reason for the aggression then ask for one. For example, 'You obviously feel very strongly about this, what in particular is concerning you?'
- If a more senior person is on the presentation team consider fielding the question to them.
- If the questioning is in danger of sidetracking discussions and decisions then 'park it'. Indicate to the individual and audience that you acknowledge the questions and the concerns behind it but intend to deal with it later – outline how that will happen and who it will involve.

Handling barriers and obstacles

Most presentations will be focused on *change* in some context. Change is always potentially painful for someone and it is important that you have thought through the implications of all of your proposals on the people involved. This will help you to recognise the obstacles and barriers that you need to overcome in order to sell your ideas, proposals or methodology.

Welcome these questions and listen for clues about the areas of concern. If you identify the customer's objections you will be in a much better position to address them directly.

Adding the sales messages

Your whole presentation is an advert for you and your organisation. To buy the message the audience must first 'buy' the presenter. That is why personal impact matters. You need to have a clear inner sense of the impression you want to create and then take the steps summarised in the checklist below.

Remember that you are working to ensure that your presentation creates a good impression, one that it is persuasive and memorable.

- Impact and first impressions are closely linked, so take care with appearance and use a firm handshake.
- Take care of your body language – upright posture, open stance, eye contact and confident hand movements are all signs of confidence and tend to get noticed.

- Positive thinking is reflected in positive appearance – control your nerves through breathing and focus externally rather than internally.
- Good preparation, clear information and well laid out support materials all create a professionalism that will ooze confidence.
- Do not feel that you need to apologise for taking people's time or for being there – you are an expert in your field and your information or offer will deliver benefits to them. Think partnership rather than adversary.
- Answer questions directly, openly and honestly – you will be remembered for the way you handle the unprepared aspects of a presentation.
- Confident presentation needs practice, so practise, practise, practise . . .

Benefits sell

If you want people to buy into your message, it is important to add the sales messages. Even when presenting information you are selling a view or concept, ideas or approach. The audience will respond to your messages if they:

- are relevant – so add in their jargon and context to help people relate to what you are saying;
- understand what is in it for them – so turn features and facts into benefits;
- can appreciate the implications of your messages – a saving of 3% per annum is less persuasive than the promise of £30k savings or the equivalent of 3000 product sales.

Look at two versions of the same presentation being delivered to a GP's surgery by a consultancy team who have been investigating the opportunity of establishing a drop-in healthcare centre in the local shopping centre.

Presentation A	*Presentation B*
Our research shows there are now over 100 such centres established across the UK. They have helped the businesses involved to attract new customers and funding. Capital invested can be expected to be paid back within three years and profitability is above average levels.	From Land's End to John O'Groats over 100 doctor's groups like yours have already taken this step – the results to date are positive. This track record will help to reassure you that the risk is not that great and the financial rewards are impressive, the equivalent of having an extra two partners in the business. The investment will be repaid in three years. The response from patients and staff in these centres is good and the profiles of the surgeries involved have been enhanced with an average of 1000 new patients registered.

Just a little attention to language, and some audience empathy, enabled presentation B to acknowledge the possible concerns about risk, staff and patient response and the surgery's image, as well as the financial details.

Listen for the 'buy' signals

While decision making can be protracted it isn't always, and in some contexts the customer will be in a position to decide quickly. Depending on your purpose this may be buying your ideas or services, but listen for the 'buy' signals and then close the sale. Many a salesperson has talked themselves out of a deal by carrying on past this point giving the buyer new objections in the latter part of their presentation.

Buy signals include questions about delivery, payment terms or implementation and suggest that the client is focusing on post-purchase issues. The domestic clients who starts talking about decoration options or delivery are at a similar stage. Don't be afraid to ask if there is any other information he needs to make a decision, or if he would like you to process the order or to check availability and begin the implementation plan.

Post-purchase dissonance

One well-documented problem for any seller of costly or risky products is *post-purchase dissonance*. This is just as likely to occur if you are selling a new idea or change strategy. This is dissatisfaction that occurs when the buyer has time to reflect on the decision. It's the dress that's still in the wardrobe because it looked better in the shop, or the car whose colour you are now having doubts about. Yesterday's decision may not always seem such a good idea with the benefit of hindsight.

If post-purchase or post-presentation dissonance may be an issue then consider a follow-up a few days later to address any queries that have arisen. Many companies follow up sales with a letter or call congratulating customers on their choice. Even the small retail outlet can encourage staff to compliment customers on their purchase. It doesn't take much reassurance to keep a customer from doubting his or her decision-making skills.

Take a few moments to think about your personal experience of post-purchase dissonance. Now think about your audiences and customers. Might it be an issue – do you ever lose sales or converts at the last hurdle? If so, think about possible post-purchase strategies.

Answers: Avoiding trouble

Some of the possible problems are quite explicit in this scenario, others require more thought. You may have picked up different and additional concerns but my list would include the following.

Possible trouble	*Action*
Not arriving on time, or arriving stressed and at the last minute	I would recommend that the team travels the night before, gets a good night's sleep and uses the morning for a last-minute review and practice.
Technology and resources – lack of preparation would make the team look less than competent	Working overseas means having adaptors for equipment like computers. I would check that the team are all equipped and have a backup of their presentation on CD.
Focus on detail – this could result in very tactical discussions that won't engage all participants all of the time	This presentation will need lots of discussion on detail. There are at least two possible strategies: ◆ send the detailed plans to each of the relevant specialists in advance of the presentation for review; ◆ plan a break-out session during the presentation, allowing each specialist to work with client representatives on the details.
The audience will be worried about logistics and catering, making them hypercritical and possibly creating a poor atmosphere	I would advise the team to recognise these genuine areas of particular concern and acknowledge it publicly. It should allocate more time to presenting details of these areas and extra time for questions. The team might also consider what else could help to reassure the client – for example, samples of the menus or tasting of planned dishes.
The likelihood of a series of ad hoc amendments	This seems a very real potential problem which could be handled by deciding on a process and presenting it for agreement at the start of the meeting. I would advise openly sharing the worries about ad hoc changes, setting up a suggestion board where ideas for changes are lodged and assessed later for possible inclusion in the plans.

▶

Possible trouble	*Action*
Four new faces on the client side. These people will need to get to know the Your Event team	Make sure there are enough information packs and background notes on the project for everyone. There is time in the presentation programme for introductions. Don't give the impression of ignoring or sidelining the new participants by focusing your attention and conversation on the people you know. Make a real point of including the new people and getting them up to speed quickly.

Answers: What would you do?

1 You could ask if the client would prefer that you came at a different time, perhaps later after the children were in bed. You can sympathise, 'It must be difficult to concentrate on these details – would you like time to review them?'

You could suggest that it might be easier to look at the plans at a table – in the kitchen or dining room – and so orchestrate a location transfer.

2 Not everyone would see this as rude, so try not to be affronted personally. I would stop the presentation and wait until the call was finished before moving on.

If in a client's venue, ask about the house rules for mobiles – perhaps one of the client team can be asked to remind participants to turn phones off. It sounds better than coming from the guest. Also remember to ensure that your team members also switch off mobiles.

3 This is more difficult. I would ask the client group whether it was best to take a five-minute break or to continue. If you continue, take the step of giving the MD a quick update of what has been missed on his or her return.

4 Do not try to present through it. Stop and continue when the test is over.

Bell tests are normally posted in reception areas, keep your eyes open and be prepared if one is planned.

5 You will have no choice but to evacuate the building. On your return start by recapping where you had got to and reminding the audience of what to expect next – you will need to negotiate new timings.

6 Another potentially tricky situation to handle. If the situation is making concentration difficult then I would wait until the next natural break in the presentation and confirm with those talking that they are following the process and check if they have questions you can help answer. If the discussions are about what is ▶

being presented then it may be that your audience might appreciate a few minutes to discuss things amongst themselves – make that suggestion.

7 You could try deflecting the questions:
   - 'We will come to that point in a moment, if you are happy to wait';
   - 'I will deal with that at the end of the presentation';
   - 'I don't want to lose the others with too much detail at this stage, I can go through that with you after the presentation'.

   You could use time as your excuse and reinforce the 'at the end' request.

8 Give them a few moments to settle down and offer to recap on what has been missed.

keep getting better

Keep moving on

As you have seen, pitches, proposals and presentations are all showcases for what you, your team or your organisation can do. In today's highly competitive business environments, where quality and performance are often expected points of differentiation are limited. Today's customers, often spoilt for choice, are as likely to be as influenced by how someone presents what they do as much as they are by real differences in the functionality of the product or service. For those who take time and effort in showcasing their offers the rewards will come in the form of increased sales, winning more business cases and higher levels of repeat clients.

This final chapter considers:

- the case for better metrics and how to use them;
- options and opportunities for learning from others and each other – building competencies and capabilities;
- feedback – potential sources and how to give and receive it effectively;
- the challenges of self-evaluation;
- tips for continual improvement.

Metrics matter

Compliments about how well you present, the clarity of your proposals or about the impact of a pitch are nice to hear but the real proof of the pudding is whether or not you get the desired results. Did you make the sale, win the repeat business or get approval for your proposal?

Whether you are working with internal or external decision-makers your success rate is what will ultimately be the best guide to your performance – metrics are objective indicators, so use them and trust them.

You saw in Chapter 3 how metrics can help to identify and prioritise the opportunities to pitch or generate proposals. With limited resources it is important that you direct your efforts when and where they are likely to have the greatest impact. In that chapter you saw that keeping more detailed metrics could provide greater insights. These same measures can also help you to evaluate your performance and provide pointers in identifying opportunities to improve.

Using the metrics

Read through the two scenarios below. If you were advising those involved, what aspects of their performance would you highlight for improvement, or what questions would you want to ask?

▶

Scenario 1

This independent production company set itself some stretching growth targets for the next two years. It knew that its reputation for delivering a good service was steadily improving, but also recognised that winning work depends on the ability to pitch effectively.

At a review meeting attendees were given following table produced by the business development manager.

Enquiries responded to – a proposal sent	*Pitches delivered*	*Contract won*
10 high-budget dramas	2	1
20 light-entertainment shows	10	6
15 location-based productions involving outside broadcasts	10	8
45 proposals in total	22 pitches in total	15 contracts won

What are your first thoughts and questions?

Compare your answers with the suggestions at the end of this chapter before moving on.

Scenario 2

A new product development team for a sportswear firm has to present the business case for each idea before investment for development and launch is available. The audience is drawn from a panel of senior managers, including at least two representatives from the product group responsible for each sport. The result over the past two years follow.

Sport	*Ideas presented*	*Approval given*
Football	14	4
Athletics	12	3
Tennis	6	4
Golf	7	4
Cricket	4	3

What aspects of the new product development's team approach might you want to review?

Check your thoughts with the suggestions given at the end of the chapter.

Comparative performance

At the very least, teams and individuals should keep track of the number of pitches, proposals and presentations along with success rates where relevant. The problem is that these ratios alone tell you relatively little. How do you know if a 1 : 4 success rate for tenders is good or bad in your sector? You need to compare it with something.

You can benchmark your performance against another team or salesperson. The comparator needs to have similar clients or offers for this to be valid. If data are available you can compare your organisation's performance with another, although in practice this competitor intelligence is unlikely to be readily available. However, you might monitor who you are typically pitching against and who gets the work – this would provide an indicator of relative win rates for key competitors.

Use your own performance over time as a benchmark.

	Pitches	*Proposals*
Year 1	1 : 5	1 : 3
Year 2	1 : 4	1 : 3
Year 3	1 : 4	1 : 4
This year	1 : 3	1 : 5

In the example above you can see that, while the team seems to be getting better at pitching, its performance with proposals is deteriorating and would be worth a more detailed analysis and review.

Take care not to look at metrics in isolation. The figures can hide significant differences in the nature of the business. For example, while 1 : 5 is less successful for proposals than the 1 : 3 ratio of Years 1 and 2, the average value of a new piece of business may have increased significantly over that time, or the market may be much more competitive than previously.

Look for patterns

To be of real help in improving performance, simple totals do not provide enough detail and you need to categorise the pitches and proposals by type of client, average value of the work, number of people in the audience or the style you use.

You are looking for patterns that allow you to say, 'We are more successful with a smaller audience and informal setting' or, 'We do better when we have more than two in our presentation team' or, 'We perform better when we take a technician with us to answer detailed queries'. The keys to success can be subtle differences in style or approach, but differences which nonetheless score with the audience and change its perceptions.

Test and measure

To improve your performance you need to be brave enough to try different approaches and styles and see if the changes make a difference. For this to be of use you need to establish 'before' and 'after' pictures – so capture the 'before' metrics, make your change and review the impact on your performance.

You will need to give the new approach some time to be sure the results are valid, so use it for five or ten pitches or presentations. As well as quantitative measures of performance, ask for qualitative feedback and compare the 'before' and 'after'.

Don't make too many changes at once or you won't be able to determine which factors are driving performance change. For example, you can decide to work on improving your empathy with the audience and introduce changes to help achieve this, but if you try to improve empathy *and* make your approach more informal then evaluation of what works and what doesn't will be harder to establish.

Be curious

Testing requires curiosity. You have to ask, 'What would happen if Neelesh took the lead for this pitch?' or, 'If we adopt a cabaret style layout for the next presentation will that pay dividends?' You need to be interested in what makes your audience tick and how you can influence their perceptions and responses.

Being curious is a valuable asset in business and it is one that too few people have, or seem to have time for. Too often we are too busy, too focused on what's next, too afraid of criticism, or just too complacent to ask the million-dollar questions:

- why did that work?
- why didn't that go better?

Unless you ask and answer these questions, any improvement in your performance is likely to be more by luck than judgement.

Being curious requires time and effort. You must make the time to review performance and ask for feedback from the team and the audience. You then need to be interested enough to examine the feedback and look for patterns that will give clues to improving your performance. You will find that analysing the successes is just as important as analysing the failures and can generate just as much insight.

Spending as much time reviewing the successes and failures will help to avoid the association of debriefs and reviews with failure. A negative focus can lead to a blame culture which won't be conducive to openness and performance improvement.

When analysing what has worked and what didn't work as well, you need to consider a number of dimensions. Firstly you should consider the content and presentation as well as the overall impression.

		Content	
		Worked	*Didn't work*
Presentation	*Worked*	Success should be yours – the right message is delivered well	Back to the drawing board – we need to understand and deliver what the customer wants
	Didn't work	The right offer let down by our presentation	The worst of all worlds

There is no point in perfecting the presentation if the content is inadequate. Similarly, there is little point tweaking the offer if the fault lies in poor presentation.

It is very easy for the salesperson or team to blame the product or price for missing a sale. This blinkered reaction prevents a serious review of the way in which you are presenting the package and will hinder your chances of improving competitive advantage. You need to look for evidence that supports your assessment of what is working or not and why. Conversely, many product-oriented organisations find it difficult even to consider that their offer may be the cause of poor sales. Effective sales depend on a package of benefit that is relevant to and valued by the client, and what worked yesterday may be less than attractive to today's customers. Open review is, once again, the antidote to the poison of product arrogance.

Debriefing performance

The analysis of what works can be done with a checklist approach to the debrief.

- Did we research the audience effectively?
- Did the offer meet the brief?
- Did we have the right technical support?
- Did the presentation have impact?
- Did we demonstrate benefits convincingly?
- Did we handle objections effectively?
- Did we respond to questions openly?
- Did we have empathy and demonstrate it?

- Did we present ourselves professionally and with impact?
- Did we give them a reason to remember us and a reason to say 'yes'?

You can create your own list of questions, which will need to be modified accordingly for pitches, proposals and presentations. The list above represents questions you want answered but if they are presented as above they will illicit yes/no answers. For more valuable feedback ask the team open questions:

- How well did we handle the questions they asked?
- How effective were the samples we gave them?

If you cannot get the team together for a verbal debrief, or if you are presenting alone, try creating a debrief questionnaire. Ask your questions but allocate 0–5 ratings as answers, and ask some open questions to capture people's impressions after the event. This discipline will make your own self-evaluation more explicit and specific.

Asking, 'What could we do better?' is a cornerstone for building continuous improvement. It does not imply poor performance but it is a characteristic of high-performing individuals and teams. It requires an open approach to learning and improvement and is based on effective feedback and review.

The whole is a sum of the parts

When you are analysing the various elements of your performance you also need to consider what you can do to make improvements. Look for the easy-to-do and high-impact options as a starting point. You might find an impact/ease grid helps you capture and categorise the aspects for improvement.

		Impact	
		High	*Low*
Ease	*Easy to do*	Prioritiy	Secondary
	Hard to do	Plan to improve	Ignore

While improving the elements of your work, do not overlook the overall impression and the effectiveness of your broad strategy. Take a step back from the detail and think about the basic approach you adopted. With the benefit of hindsight, was it right or could it have been better? Try to put yourself in the audience's shoes – what words would they use to describe you. Review this against the impression you had planned to create. Identify the gaps and differences and consider how best to address these in future.

Your own worst critic

The very best presenters and sales teams get things wrong, and there are always things that could have been done better. It is very easy to become your own worst critic and to turn what should be an opportunity for learning and improving into a process that threatens confidence levels and future performance. If this is a danger then get into the habit of matching each opportunity for improvement with an aspect that was improved or went well.

Focus on what could be better, not on what went wrong.

Feedback

Crucial to continuous improvement is feedback. If you want to improve your own performance you need to become a proactive seeker of feedback and be alert to its various sources open to you. You may be surprised by the number of options.

- **Audience response** – perhaps the most direct, and in some ways obvious, source of feedback.
- **Listen to people's questions** – what the audience asks can provide considerable insight into the content's clarity, or lack of it, when you were explaining concepts, findings or costings, etc. If some haven't heard or understood, revisit what you were saying and how you were saying it.
- **Ask them directly** – you can ask an audience whether or not you have made a point clearly, or if it has understood your proposal.
- **Watch the body language** – observation is an excellent source of feedback. Is the audience engaged, nodding, leaning forward or are some looking bored and glancing at their watches?
- **Do they say 'yes'?** – those outcome metrics are a strong indicator of your performance. If you achieve your objectives then the pitch or presentation was pretty effective. That doesn't mean you should become complacent, nor indeed that there isn't room for improvement.
- **Third-party feedback** – in many contexts it is possible to get feedback from an observer. Look for someone who is neither part of the team nor part of the audience, if at all possible. Make sure you brief this observer carefully. He or she needs to know what you are looking for and needs a framework for how to benchmark your performance. Develop a checklist and scoring system for the observer, perhaps based on the checklist suggested earlier in this chapter. Third-

party observers can be particularly useful at the rehearsal and practice stage. If they take on the role of the audience they provide a more realistic setting – not quite as adrenaline boosting as the real thing, but more useful than practising in an empty room.

Use third parties as non-expert reviewers of written proposals. Encourage them to ask the dumb questions. Test them to check what key messages they have taken from the documentation and how well they have understood complex material.

- **Self-assessment** – the dangers of becoming your own worst critic have already been highlighted, but that does not invalidate the potential for self-assessment. This opportunity is as useful for individuals as for teams. To be of value the process of self-assessment needs to be structured and honest. Lay down your own rules. You might like to start with these:
  - match good with bad to keep your assessment balanced;
  - never judge performance without evidence to support it – you have to be able to justify;
  - have a checklist of factors/criteria that you are assessing the performance against;
  - review and assess regularly so it becomes a familiar and comfortable process;
  - use your evaluation positively so it is followed up with ideas for improvement;
  - focus on things you can change and do something about;
  - celebrate the improvements and successes.

  You can video presentations or rehearsals and record question and answer sessions. It can be a shock seeing and hearing yourself if you aren't used to it, but any bad presentation habits will be only too apparent to you.

Audio recording is easy to do and is a useful technique when practising a speech or longer presentations. It forces you to listen, without the distraction of the visual input. Check your diction for clarity and your modulation. Do you use emphasis and variation in tone to make the content interesting? If you find yourself nodding off after five minutes then get working on your delivery style.

- **Reviewing feedback** – on paper, the idea of feedback seems sensible and logical but it isn't always that easy to receive it graciously or enthusiastically. Positive comments can easily embarrass and the negative can hurt or feel like unfair criticism. Accept the fact that not everyone gives feedback well. It is a difficult thing to do, but usually it is well-intentioned.

Make a point of ensuring that your team are all trained to give and receive feedback constructively.

Think about how feedback will help to improve your skills and performance – it is for your benefit.

Think about the last time you were on the receiving end of feedback. As you look at the points in this checklist assess how well you did and make a note of how you can improve your performance in this area.

- Be open to feedback. When offered it, take it – the beneficiary will be you.
- Listen carefully to what is said.
- Clarify anything you do not understand, or ask for examples of relevant instances.
- Try not to become defensive or to overreact.
- Listen to the positive comments as well as the negative. Accept both maturely, and say thank you.
- Discuss suggestions for improving performance.
- Positively seek further feedback so you can monitor if your performance is improving.
- Empathise with the person giving feedback – he or she won't want to feel you are upset or offended.

To help you to make a more objective assessment of how well you take feedback, consider your recent pitching or presenting activities. How have you changed or modified your approach over this time as a result of feedback you have received?

If you haven't, or aren't sure, then you need to take a good look at your own attitude to continuous improvement. Take proactive steps to get feedback and then plan positive action to implement changes.

Giving feedback

Receiving feedback can be hard but so can giving it. If you work as part of a team you need to build your skills in the giving as well as the receiving. The first problem with feedback is that many people expect it to involve criticism – this is often because of poor past experience. In reality, feedback and criticism are very different – or should be.

If you find yourself on the receiving end of criticism masquerading as feedback then use the feedback from this following activity to structure some feedback of your own.

As the giver of feedback, it is always important to be sensitive as to how it might be taken. In the context of public performance, which is a key part of pitches and presentations, you need to be particularly careful with people's self-confidence – it can be fragile.

Describing the difference

Look at these pairs of descriptions. One of them characterises feedback – so label it with an F. The other represents criticism so label it C. By the end you should have a clear distinction between them.

Description A	*C/F*	*Description B*	*C/F*
Frequent		Rare	
One-sided		Balanced	
Problem-focused		Solution-focused	
Performance-focused		Person-focused	
Direct and clear		Vague and ambiguous	
Judgemental		Descriptive	
Imposed		Offered	
Not owned, 'we'		Owned, 'I'	

You can check your classifications with the suggestions at the end of this chapter.

Good feedback in practice

You have a description of good feedback. You can now consider the examples below to see how you might deliver good feedback in practice.

- **Timing** – good feedback is regular not occasional. If it is routine it seems less threatening. It needs to be given soon after an event – not five minutes after leaving the client's building but perhaps the next day. You want people to have time to reflect but not so long they forget the details.
- **Ownership** – feedback must be owned by the giver, based on his or her observations and supported by evidence.
  - Everyone thought your attitude was negative. ✗
  - I noticed that your body language during Jo's presentation was not very positive – you were sat back and made no eye contact ✓
- **Clarity** – if feedback is to inform performance, what needs improving must be clear – there must be no confusion. That means clear, specific and direct.
  - Well, it's fairly clear your outfit was inappropriate. ✗
  - It is important that the whole team dresses in a way that reflects the organisation's values – jeans and T-shirts will need to be replaced by smart casual slacks and shirts. ✓

- **Invited** – good feedback should never be imposed, it should be offered. The receiver has the right to refuse it, and that needs to be respected. In a positive and trusting working environment you would expect feedback to be valued and welcomed. If it isn't, you might look at the culture of your team.
  - Let me just tell you what I think would have made that better. ✗
  - Would you like some feedback on how you might add more impact to future presentations? ✓
- **Focused on performance and solutions** – the focus of the feedback needs to be on what happened and how it can be improved.
  - In the question and answer session you came across as a bully and it really upset the rest of the team. ✗
  - By jumping in to answer all the questions you sidelined your colleagues and undermined the sense of team we were trying to portray. Why don't you consider taking the role of chair next time and field the questions to the others as appropriate? ✓
- **Be descriptive** – judgemental statements and labelling, as in the bullying example above, are open to misinterpretation. What you mean by autocratic or dynamic may not mirror my impression. If you are more specific and descriptive there is more likely to be a clear understanding of what was meant.
  - Your presentation style is too melodramatic. 
  - You know when you were presenting the background to the client's problem, you tended to leave extra long pauses to add effect. It made the problems seem even more serious than they are – it seemed to me that you almost scared the directors. ✓
- **Add balance** – you can try the 'two for one' rule to ensure balance. One-sided feedback sounds like criticism.
  - Those slides were too busy and there were too many of them. 
  - I thought the way that you used title slides to structure the arguments worked really well and the choice of colours was a great improvement on last time. Now perhaps we should look at reducing the content and keeping the messages simple. ✓

Barriers to feedback

Poor giving or receiving of feedback will reduce your – and your organisation's – ability to improve. So problems need to be tackled and barriers overcome. Try to establish what people's perceptions and problems are and what their experiences have been. Try using an 'expectations, hopes and fears' exercise with the team. Working in twos or threes members can brainstorm under these headings and then share their views.

- Establish the ground rules.
- Make sure everyone knows how to give good feedback and receive it.

- Practise the process in a safe environment.
- Ask for feedback on how it is going.
- Use this checklist to help you monitor your feedback-giving:
  - Offer feedback – don't force it on people.
  - Be specific and descriptive.
  - Be balanced – highlight the good as well as the bad. Add evidence to support your comments.
  - Focus on what people did, not who they are – and don't compare individuals.
  - Be supportive and encourage responses to your comments – you need dialogue.
  - Be reasonable – people can only absorb so much at a time.
  - Be constructive – give suggestions for improvement.
  - Do not apologise for giving feedback.
- Give feedback as soon after the pitch or presentation as possible.
- Make a habit of *always* providing feedback – you will get better at it and it will become an expected part of the process.

Using open questions

Open questions really help in the process of giving feedback. This method avoids the feeling of lecturing that can result from an unbroken monologue of commentary. Open questions demand an extended response and so the listener has to engage with the discussion, think about the response and venture an opinion. This encourages people to talk freely – their active participation takes away the pressure they might feel if they perceive the process as you passing judgement on their performance.

Turning feedback into open questions

Look at the following examples of feedback. Think about how each statement might be effectively turned into an open question.

1 You didn't seem to understand the client's brief very well.
2 You were distracted and inattentive throughout the process.
3 You were responsible for ensuring that the samples were available and you let us down.
4 You were too willing to offer them a discount.
5 That presentation came across as unrehearsed.
6 The audience were not engaged from the first minutes.

Check your ideas against those suggested at the end of the chapter.

Continual improvement

If you and your team want to get better and better, you need to have an improvement strategy and a plan for implementing it. Treat this as a separate but parallel process when preparing for a specific presentation. Assume there is always room for improvement and agree that every pitch or presentation will be better than the last. Use feedback and analysis to help to identify the aspects of improvement that would have the biggest impact on performance.

Don't be afraid of structured personal development. This doesn't need to be formal training – though that can help. Find colleagues who are good presenters or who have graphics and design skills, and ask for coaching. Use team meetings to practise, and watch and evaluate politicians and orators as they speak. Remember to celebrate the improvements and have milestones to keep the team motivated and focused.

A final word

I hope you have found many of the ideas and tips in this book of practical help. As always, the challenge now is for you to take and use that learning. That involves time and effort. It might mean that you need to give some straightforward feedback to others. There will be a million reasons to put changes off. So my final tips:

- Go back to the chapter where you calculated the business benefits of getting better. Visualise the extra commission, resources or profit that those extra sales represent.
- Don't try to improve everything at once – be selective and use analysis to help you focus and use resources where they will have the most impact.
- When you start to see the results, keep striving for continual improvement.
- Let me know how you get on and what you thought of the book – I would welcome your feedback (angela@tacticsconsultancy.com).

Answers: Using the metrics

Scenario 1

Although metrics are useful, they don't tell the whole story and will often raise as many questions as answers. Faced with these numbers I would want to do the following.

- Find out the extent to which reputation and track record was influencing the different success rates in these three sectors of work.
- Analyse the different characteristics of the three sectors in terms of average contract values, format or type of brief given, and the dynamics and approach to choosing suppliers. For example, if the drama producers are more formal in their

approach it may indicate poorer performance in tender-style proposals and formal pitching. It is possible there is a one-size-fits-all approach that isn't recognising client differences.

- Try to benchmark performance against that of other companies to assess how well or poorly you compare.
- I would want to focus initially on improving proposals where performance varies from 1 : 5 success for drama, to a high of 2 : 3 for location-based work. Pitches have a better track record with a 1 : 2 rate being the lowest and 4 : 5 the highest.

Scenario 2

The first observation is that there are significantly more ideas presented for football and athletics, yet the success rate is lower. I would want to ask:

- is the team allocating its resources in the most effective area and is it being self-critical enough in deciding what to present in the areas of football and athletics;
- are the needs of the product managers and the differences between the sports fully understood and reflected in the various presentations made;
- are there other constraints and influences – for example, is each product group limited to a maximum of four new launches per annum?

Customer research and feedback is key to improving this performance – detailed analysis of why ideas are rejected would help the development team to focus its resources more effectively.

Answers: Describing the difference

F: regular, balanced, solution-focused, performance-focused, direct and clear, descriptive, offered, owned

C: rare, one-sided, problem-focused, person-focused, judgemental, imposed, not owned.

Answers: Turning feedback into open questions

You might have come up with questions like these.

1 Could you describe or explain to me how you went about familiarising yourself with the client's brief?
2 How did you feel during that presentation?
3 What do you think went wrong with the organisation of the samples?
4 Can you tell me why you offered a discount so early in the negotiation?
5 Tell me about the way in which you rehearsed or prepared for this presentation.
6 How do you think the audience felt about what you had to say?

index